SIGNIFICANT DECISIONS
OF THE SUPREME COURT
1973-74 Term

SIGNIFICANT DECISIONS OF THE SUPREME COURT
1973-74 Term

Bruce E. Fein

American Enterprise Institute for Public Policy Research
Washington, D.C.

Bruce E. Fein, a graduate of Harvard Law School and a former clerk to a U.S. district judge, is a member of the California Bar and the American Bar Association.

ISBN 0-8447-3176-5

Domestic Affairs Study 36, October 1975

Library of Congress Catalog Card L.C. 75-21832

Printed in the United States of America

CONTENTS

1
OVERVIEW

Principal Decisions

Watergate Tapes. The Supreme Court's most dramatic decision during the 1973–74 term was rendered in the case of *United States* v. *Nixon*, which ultimately led to the resignation of the President two weeks later. In a unanimous opinion written by Chief Justice Burger, the Court ordered President Nixon to produce sixty-four tape recordings for possible use in the trial of six Watergate defendants.

The stage was set for the Court's historic decision when District Judge John Sirica ordered President Nixon to disclose the contents of the tapes to him for in camera inspection. Paralleling this decision was the House Judiciary Committee investigation to determine whether the President should be impeached. President Nixon appealed Judge Sirica's decision to the court of appeals. The Supreme Court then granted Special Prosecutor Leon Jaworski's request to review the case immediately on the ground that it presented issues of "imperative public importance." The Court has granted direct review of district court decisions in only a handful of cases.

On 24 July 1974, the same day that the House Judiciary Committee began televising the final stages of its impeachment proceedings, the Supreme Court affirmed Judge Sirica's decision, and the tapes subsequently were delivered to the Court. On 5 August, the White House publicly revealed information from one of the tapes turned over to Judge Sirica. This action prompted strong congressional demands for the President's resignation or immediate impeachment, and the President resigned on 9 August 1974.

Bombing of Cambodia. Even before the formal beginning of its 1973–74 term, the Court was involved in political controversy in connection with the bombing of Cambodia. In July 1973, a federal district judge ruled that the United States military air operations over Cambodia had not been authorized by Congress and were thus unconstitutional. The district court permanently enjoined the secretary of defense, the acting secretary of the Air Force, and the deputy secretary of defense from "participating in any way in military activities in or over Cambodia or releasing any bombs which may fall in Cambodia." The court of appeals stayed the district court order pending a decision on the appeal. The plaintiffs in the case applied to Justice Marshall to stay the order of the court of appeals, thereby reinstating the effectiveness of the district court's injunction. Justice Marshall denied the application on 1 August 1973.[1] As permitted by rule 50 of the Supreme Court, the plaintiffs then applied to Justice Douglas for a stay, which was granted on 4 August.[2] The same day, Justice Marshall, acting with the concurrence of all members of the Court except Justice Douglas, stayed the order of the district court.[3]

The court of appeals ultimately reversed the district court's ruling on the grounds that (1) the question of the legality of the bombing of Cambodia was a nonjusticiable political question, (2) Congress had authorized the bombing, and (3) the plaintiffs lacked standing to challenge the legality of the bombing.[4] The Supreme Court declined to review the decision of the court of appeals.[5] In taking that action, the Supreme Court seems to have ruled out the possibility that it will make any decision on the merits concerning the legality of United States military involvement in Southeast Asia during the past decade.

Busing. Except for the rulings on Cambodia bombing and in the Watergate tapes case, the Supreme Court decision having greatest political impact concerned busing. The Court ruled that a plan to desegregate Detroit public schools by interdistrict busing between inner-city, primarily black schools and predominantly white suburban school districts was improper. That decision may have defused a strong congressional move to restrict severely the power of federal courts to order busing as a desegregation remedy.

Voting Alignments

The Court's 1973–74 term suggested the beginning of a notable trend

[1]Holtzman v. Schlesinger, 414 U.S. 1304 (1973).
[2]Holtzman v. Schlesinger, 414 U.S. 1316 (1973).
[3]Schlesinger v. Holtzman, 414 U.S. 1321 (1973).
[4]Holtzman v. Schlesinger, 484 F.2d 1307 (2d Cir. 1973).
[5]416 U.S. 936 (1974).

in voting alignments. Justice Powell, a Nixon appointee, voted in some significant cases with the justices generally described as "liberals."[6] For example, he joined with the liberal justices in decisions holding unconstitutional flag desecration prosecutions[7] and recognizing a right to jury trial in certain contempt cases.[8] He joined them in dissenting from a decision denying newsmen a right to interview prisoners.[9]

The Court now seems to be divided into three groups. The votes of Justices Burger, Blackmun, and Rehnquist are generally classified as conservative, Justices Douglas, Brennan, and Marshall tend to take the liberal view, and Justices Stewart, White, and Powell are considered by some as moderate swing votes but are generally conservative on criminal law issues.

As in its 1972–73 term, many of the Court's most important cases were decided by 5–4 votes. Significant issues concerning cross-district busing,[10] standing,[11] the right to recover welfare benefits illegally withheld,[12] antitrust laws,[13] due process,[14] libel,[15] and political advertising[16] were all decided by this margin. The Court generally followed a conservative course in criminal law cases, but its decisions in other areas revealed no doctrinal consistency. The prevailing tendency of the "Burger Court" has been rejection of the course followed by the "Warren Court," which thrust itself into various highly controversial issues.

The "Warren Court" created great political controversy in its reapportionment decisions establishing and expanding the one-person, one-vote rule.[17] The "Burger Court," in contrast, has narrowed

---

[6]The terms "liberal," "moderate," and "conservative" are used here in a popular political sense.

[7]Smith v. Goguen, 415 U.S. 566 (1974); Spence v. Washington, 418 U.S. 405 (1974).

[8]Codispoti v. Pennsylvania, 418 U.S. 506 (1974).

[9]Pell v. Procunier, 417 U.S. 817 (1974).

[10]Milliken v. Bradley, 418 U.S. 717 (1974).

[11]United States v. Richardson, 418 U.S. 166 (1974).

[12]Edelman v. Jordan, 415 U.S. 651 (1974).

[13]United States v. General Dynamics Corp., 415 U.S. 486 (1974); United States v. Connecticut National Bank, 418 U.S. 656 (1974).

[14]Mitchell v. W. T. Grant, 416 U.S. 600 (1974).

[15]Gertz v. Welch, Inc., 418 U.S. 323 (1974).

[16]Lehman v. Shaker Heights, 418 U.S. 298 (1974).

[17]See Baker v. Carr, 369 U.S. 186 (1962); Reynolds v. Sims, 377 U.S. 533 (1964); Wesberry v. Sanders, 376 U.S. 1 (1964); Avery v. Midland County, 390 U.S. 474 (1968).

the application[18] of those cases and has provided the states with considerably more constitutional leeway in reapportioning their legislatures.[19] The "Warren Court" also decided the landmark case of *Miranda* v. *Arizona*, 384 U.S. 436 (1966), which some regard as a symbol of the judiciary constitutionally shackling reasonable law enforcement efforts. The "Burger Court" has limited the impact of *Miranda*.[20] The "Warren Court" seemed willing to decide issues which many thought were outside the proper purview of the federal judiciary.[21] The "Burger Court," on the other hand, has avoided reaching the merits of several potentially controversial decisions.[22] Nevertheless, the contrast between the two courts should not be overemphasized. It reveals more a change of judicial mood than a clear turn of judicial direction. The "Burger Court," it should be noted, has produced both the capital punishment and abortion decisions.[23]

Federal Rules of Evidence

Pursuant to various enabling acts, the Supreme Court in 1972 promulgated the Federal Rules of Evidence, which were to take effect 1 July 1973. One of the proposed rules, rule 509, provided that the government could refuse to give evidence "upon a showing of reasonable likelihood of danger that the evidence will disclose a secret of state or official information. . . ." A state secret was defined as a "governmental secret relating to the national defense or international relations of the United States." Official information was defined as information whose disclosure would adversely affect the public interest. It would include law enforcement investigatory files, intragovernmental opinions, and information not disclosable under the Freedom of Information Act. Partly in response to controversy surrounding rule 509, Congress enacted a statute on 30 March 1973 delaying the effective date of the Federal Rules of Evidence until Congress affirmatively approved them.

[18]See Sayler Land Co. v. Tulare Water District, 410 U.S. 719 (1973); Associated Enterprises, Inc. v. Toltec Watershed Improvement District, 410 U.S. 743 (1973).
[19]Compare Swann v. Adams, 385 U.S. 440 (1967) with Mahan v. Howell, 410 U.S. 315 (1973) and Gaffney v. Cummings, 412 U.S. 735 (1973).
[20]See Harris v. New York, 401 U.S. 222 (1971); Michigan v. Tucker, 417 U.S. 433 (1974).
[21]Many scholars believed that the issues decided in the reapportionment cases and Powell v. McCormack, 395 U.S. 486 (1969) raised nonjusticiable political questions.
[22]See Schlesinger v. Reservists Committee to Stop the War, 418 U.S. 208 (1974); United States v. Richardson, 418 U.S. 166 (1974); DeFunis v. Odegaard, 416 U.S. 312 (1974).
[23]Furman v. Georgia, 408 U.S. 238 (1972); Roe v. Wade, 410 U.S. 113 (1973); Doe v. Bolton, 410 U.S. 179 (1973).

Table 1
BACKGROUND OF SUPREME COURT JUSTICES, 1973–74 TERM

Justice	Nominating President	Date Seated
Warren E. Burger, Chief Justice	Richard M. Nixon	23 June 1969
William O. Douglas	Franklin D. Roosevelt	17 April 1939[a]
William J. Brennan, Jr.	Dwight D. Eisenhower	16 October 1956
Potter Stewart	Dwight D. Eisenhower	14 October 1958
Byron R. White	John F. Kennedy	16 April 1962
Thurgood Marshall	Lyndon B. Johnson	2 October 1967
Harry A. Blackmun	Richard M. Nixon	9 June 1970
Lewis F. Powell, Jr.	Richard M. Nixon	7 January 1972
William H. Rehnquist	Richard M. Nixon	7 January 1972

[a] In October 1973 Justice Douglas became the longest sitting justice in the history of the Supreme Court.

In February 1974, the House of Representatives approved a bill (H.R. 5463) that would establish rules of evidence for United States courts and magistrates. The bill differed substantially from the Federal Rules of Evidence promulgated by the Supreme Court. In particular, the bill deleted the privilege created for state secrets and official information in rule 509. It provided instead that the government's privilege of withholding evidence "shall be governed by the principles of the common law as they may be interpreted by the courts of the United States in light of reason and experience." The Senate adopted the House treatment of state secrets, and the Federal Rules of Evidence became law on 2 January 1975 (Public Law 93–595).

1973–74 Statistics

The caseload of the Supreme Court jumped to a new record this term with a total of 5,079 cases on the docket. The Court produced a record 161 decisions with full opinions, and disposed of a record 3,876 cases, leaving 1,203 cases on the docket for the next term. Statistics reflecting the work of individual justices and the Court as a whole may be found in Tables 1 through 4.

Table 2

NUMBER OF PRINTED OPINIONS AND MEMORANDA FILED DURING 1972 AND 1973 OCTOBER TERMS

Justices	Opinions of the Court		Concurring Opinions[a]		Dissenting Opinions		Separate Opinions		Individual Totals	
	1972	1973	1972	1973	1972	1973	1972	1973	1972	1973
Burger (Chief Justice)	19	14	6	0	6	4	2	1	33	19
Douglas	16	14	4	6	41	43	12	2	73	65
Brennan	13	15	3	1	26	20	1	1	43	37
Stewart	16	17	8	6	12	7	1	4	37	34
White	17	19	4	8	12	12	2	1	35	40
Marshall	12	13	6	3	17	17	4	4	39	37
Blackmun	14	15	9	7	3	7	5	1	31	30
Powell	17	16	5	6	6	4	3	8	31	34
Rehnquist	16	17	1	3	17	11	1	1	35	32
Total	140	140	46	40	140	125	31	23	357	328

a Includes opinions concurring in part and dissenting in part.

Note: There were 17 per curiam opinions among the 18 cases argued during the 1972 October term. During the 1973 October term, there were 8 per curiam opinions out of 8 cases disposed of. Memorandum opinions of individual justices in chamber matters, dissenting to per curiams in cases not argued, on the denial of petitions for certiorari, and so on, are not included in the above figures. Of the 170 cases argued during the 1973 October term, 161 were decided by signed opinions and 8 by per curiam opinions. One case was set for reargument.

Source: Compilation by Clerk of the Supreme Court, 43 U.S.L.W. 3086 (13 August 1974).

Table 3

CASES FILED, DISPOSED OF, AND REMAINING ON DOCKETS AT CONCLUSION OF 1971, 1972, AND 1973 OCTOBER TERMS

Type of Case	On Dockets	Disposed of during Terms	Remaining on Dockets
Original			
1971	18	8	10
1972	21	8	13
1973	14	4	10
Appellate			
1971	2070	1628	442
1972	2183	1771	412
1973	2480	1868	612
Miscellaneous			
1971	2445	2009	436
1972	2436	1969	467
1973	2585	2004	581
Totals			
1971	4533	3645	888
1972	4640	3748	892
1973	5079	3876	1203

Source: Same as for Table 2.

Table 4

DISPOSITION OF CASES, 1971, 1972, AND 1973 OCTOBER TERMS

Number of Cases	1971 Term	1972 Term	1973 Term
Argued during term	177[a]	177	170
Disposed of by full opinions	(143)	(159)	(161)
Disposed of by per curiam opinions	(24)[b]	(18)	(8)
Set for reargument	(9)[c]	0	(1)
Granted review during term	163[d]	154	183
Reviewed and decided without oral argument	286	265	188
Total to be available for argument at outset of following term	99	76	89

[a] Includes No. 9 Original (Pending).
[b] Includes A-483 and No. 50 Original.
[c] Includes four cases that were reargued in the 1971 October term.
[d] Includes A-483 and No. 9 Original.

Source: Same as for Table 2.

2

SUMMARIES OF SIGNIFICANT DECISIONS

Each of the following sections presents a brief general survey of the work of the Court in a given area of law followed by a case-by-case summary of the significant cases in that area. The majority opinion is summarized except in those few cases in which a majority of the justices did not join in any one opinion. In such cases, the plurality opinion is summarized.

Executive Privilege

The case of *United States* v. *Nixon* was the first instance in which the Court sketched the parameters of executive privilege while giving the privilege constitutional roots. Because the Court rejected President Nixon's claim of absolute executive privilege and ordered his compliance with the special prosecutor's subpoena, the scope of executive privilege recognized by the Court's decision was generally overlooked. The decision, although ultimately leading to President Nixon's resignation, may nevertheless have strengthened presidential powers vis-à-vis Congress.

United States v. *Nixon* established the following constitutional propositions: first, that presidential claims of executive privilege are subject to judicial review; second, that executive privilege asserted to protect a generalized interest in the confidentiality of presidential communications, though entitled to great respect, must yield to other important constitutional interests such as the specific need for evidence in a criminal trial. The decision indicated that executive privilege asserted to protect the national security would be entitled to greater deference than privilege based upon confidentiality.

Congressional inquiries into conduct in some part of the executive branch are virtually ongoing. Congressional oversight is one of the most effective ways in which Congress can ensure that the executive branch is held accountable for its actions. In the course of congressional hearings, information requested by a congressional committee is sometimes denied by the executive branch. The committee may deem the information essential for a determination of whether the executive is acting in accordance with statutory mandates. Nevertheless, the Court's decision in *United States* v. *Nixon* tends to indicate that a committee would not prevail in a lawsuit brought to compel production of such information over a claim of executive privilege based upon either confidentiality or national security.

In ordering the President to disclose tapes and documents concerning confidential conversations, the Court noted that presidential advisors are unlikely to give uncandid advice simply because there is a remote possibility that their comments will be needed as evidence in a criminal trial. If congressional committees could compel disclosure of presidential communications, the probability of loss of candor is much higher, because congressional demands for such information are frequent. That potential loss of uninhibited advice, in the Court's view, might outweigh the congressional need for information. The Court's decision indicates that Congress would have even less success when attempting to obtain information over a presidential claim of privilege based upon national security. Thus, this decision may have its greatest and most enduring impact upon the power of Congress to investigate the executive branch.

United States v. Nixon, 418 U.S. 683 (1974)

Facts: Pursuant to rule 17(c) of the Federal Rules of Criminal Procedure, Special Prosecutor Leon Jaworski issued a subpoena directing the President to produce sixty-four tape recordings and documents relating to his conversations with aides and advisors for use in the so-called Watergate cover-up trial. The President moved to quash the subpoena on the grounds that (1) the refusal to turn over the tapes and documents had created an intrabranch dispute between a subordinate and superior officer of the executive branch that was not subject to judicial resolution, (2) the subpoena failed to meet the requirements of rule 17(c), and (3) the President possesses an absolute executive privilege to keep confidential presidential communications secret. The district court denied the motion to quash and ordered the President to submit the subpoenaed tapes and documents for in camera review for the purpose of separating irrelevant information from relevant evidence to be used at the trial. The President appealed to the court of appeals. However, because of the importance of the case, the Supreme Court granted certiorari without waiting for a decision from the court of appeals.

Question: Must the President comply with the special prosecutor's subpoena?

Decision: Yes. Opinion by Chief Justice Burger. Vote: 8–0. Rehnquist did not participate.

Reasons: The initial question was whether the district court order was appealable and was thus ready for review in the Supreme Court. The U.S. Code (28 U.S. Code, 1291) permits appeals only from "final decisions of the district courts." It has been repeatedly held that an order denying a motion to quash a subpoena duces tecum is not a final decision and hence not appealable unless the party resisting the subpoena puts himself in contempt of the order.

> To require a President of the United States to place himself in the posture of disobeying an order of a court merely to trigger the procedural mechanism for review of the ruling would be unseemly, and present an unnecessary occasion for constitutional confrontation between two branches of the Government. . . . [A] federal judge should not be placed in the posture of issuing a citation to a President simply in order to invoke review. The issue whether a President can be cited for contempt could itself engender protracted litigation, and would further delay both review on the merits of his claim of privilege and the ultimate termination of the underlying criminal action for which his evidence is sought. These considerations lead us to conclude that the order of the District Court was an appealable order.

Turning to the issue of justiciability, the Court noted that the attorney general, by regulation, had authorized the special prosecutor to contest the invocation of executive privilege in connection with the prosecution of Watergate and related cases. Additionally, that regulation granted the special prosecutor total independence from the attorney general in the discharge of his duties and provided that he would not be removed "except for extraordinary improprieties. . . ." The executive branch is bound by the regulation as long as it remains in force. The dispute between the special prosecutor and the President arose in the regular course of a federal criminal prosecution and is within the traditional scope of the federal judicial power:

> In light of the uniqueness of the setting in which the conflict arises, the fact that both parties are officers of the Executive Branch cannot be viewed as a barrier to justiciability. It

would be inconsistent with the applicable law and regulation, and the unique facts of this case to conclude other than that the Special Prosecutor has standing to bring this action and that a justiciable controversy is presented for decision.

The subpoena clearly met the requirements of rule 17(c) which permits a court to order the production of evidence prior to trial. Rule 17(c) requires the party seeking the evidence to show the following:

(1) that the documents are evidentiary and relevant; (2) that they are not otherwise procurable reasonably in advance of trial by exercise of due diligence; (3) that the party cannot properly prepare for trial without such production and inspection in advance of trial and that the failure to obtain such inspection may tend unreasonably to delay the trial; and (4) that the application is made in good faith and is not intended as a general "fishing expedition."

The record in this case shows that the special prosecutor satisfied these four requirements.

It was argued, nevertheless, that the subpoena should be quashed, because (1) the separation of powers doctrine precludes judicial review of a President's claim of executive privilege and (2) in any event the Court should uphold the claim of privilege over the subpoena. With regard to the first contention, the Court concluded that the federal judicial power could not be shared with the President: "Any other conclusion would be contrary to the basic concept of separation of powers and the checks and balances that flow from the scheme of a tripartite government. . . . We therefore reaffirm that it is 'emphatically the province and the duty' of this Court 'to say what the law is' with respect to the claim of privilege presented in this case."

In connection with the second contention, the Court stated that there exists a "valid need for protection of communications between high Government officials and those who advise and assist them in the performance of their manifold duties. . . ." Continuing, the Court reasoned that

[h]uman experience teaches that those who expect public dissemination of their remarks may well temper candor with a concern for appearances and for their own interests to the detriment of the decision-making process. Whatever the nature of the privilege of confidentiality of Presidential communications in the exercise of Art. II powers, the privilege can be said to derive from the supremacy of each branch within its own assigned area of constitutional duties. . . .

However, neither the doctrine of separation of powers, nor the need for confidentiality of high level communications, without more, can sustain an absolute, unqualified Presidential privilege of immunity from judicial process under all circumstances. . . . [W]hen the privilege depends solely on the broad, undifferentiated claim of public interest in the confidentiality of such conversations, a confrontation with other values arises. . . .

The Court observed that unqualified executive privilege would impede the primary constitutional duty of the judicial branch to do justice in criminal prosecutions. It reasoned that the interest in maintaining the integrity of the judicial system outweighed the President's substantial interest·in preserving confidentiality. A President's advisors, the Court thought, were unlikely " to temper the candor of their remarks by the infrequent occasions of disclosure because of the possibility that such conversations will be called for in the context of a criminal prosecution." Accordingly, the Court ruled that "when the ground for asserting privilege as to subpoenaed materials sought for use in a criminal trial is based only on the generalized interest in confidentiality, it cannot prevail over the fundamental demands of due process of law in the fair administration of criminal justice."

Criminal Law: Powers of the Police and Prosecutors

With regard to criminal law issues, the "Burger Court" has generally taken a more conservative stance than the "Warren Court." The Burger Court has narrowed the impact of many Warren Court decisions that limited investigatory powers and established certain rights for the accused, but it has not overruled those decisions.[1] In some areas of criminal law the Burger Court has expanded the rights of the accused.[2] However, in cases concerning Fourth Amendment protections against unreasonable searches and seizures, the Burger Court has shown an increasing trend to depart from the reasoning and spirit of the Warren

[1]Compare Miranda v. Arizona, 384 U.S. 436 (1966), in which the Warren Court held that statements made by an accused could not be used at trial unless he had been informed of his legal right to counsel and to remain silent, with Harris v. New York, 401 U.S. 222 (1970), in which the Burger Court held that statements made by an accused who had not received his so-called Miranda warnings could be used to impeach his credibility if he testified in his own defense. Also compare United States v. Wade, 388 U.S. 218 (1967), in which the Warren Court held that an accused has a right to counsel during a line-up, with Kirby v. Illinois, 406 U.S. 682 (1972), in which the Burger Court held that an accused has a right to counsel only during line-ups that occur after the accused is formally charged.
[2]See, for example, Argersinger v. Hamlin, 407 U.S. 25 (1972), in which the Court held that an indigent has a right to free counsel in any criminal case that might result in imprisonment.

Court's decisions. Part of the explanation for this trend is the great dissatisfaction on the part of several of the justices with the so-called exclusionary rule which prohibits the use of evidence obtained in violation of the accused's Fourth Amendment rights. It may seem especially foolish to appellate justices to overturn a conviction based upon trustworthy and reliable evidence on the ground that some of the evidence was obtained in violation of the Fourth Amendment. However, a primary rationale for the exclusionary rule is that it deters police violations of the Fourth Amendment.

The Burger Court's dissatisfaction with the exclusionary rule seems to be one reason for its having paid little deference to the general Fourth Amendment requirement that warrants be obtained to justify a search and having ruled in favor of police and prosecutors on most important Fourth Amendment issues decided during the last four terms.[3] During the 1973–74 term, the Court made the following rulings:

—The exclusionary rule does not apply to grand jury proceedings.

—Police may thoroughly search an individual under custodial

---

[3]See Hill v. California, 401 U.S. 797 (1971), in which warrantless search of an apartment was held legal; United States v. White, 401 U.S. 745 (1971), in which it was held that the Fourth Amendment permits government agents to monitor the statements made by a suspect to an informer; Wyman v. James, 400 U.S. 309 (1971), in which it was held that requiring home visits by caseworkers as a condition to receiving welfare does not violate the Fourth Amendment; United States v. Harriss, 403 U.S. 573 (1971), in which it was held that a search warrant issued partially in reliance upon a policeman's knowledge of a suspect's criminal reputation was based upon probable cause; Adams v. Williams, 407 U.S. 143 (1972), in which it was held that police may "stop and frisk" a suspicious person on the basis of an informant's tip; United States v. Biswell, 406 U.S. 311 (1972), in which the Court held that warrantless searches of business premises to enforce gun control laws are lawful; Cady v. Dombrowski, 413 U.S. 433 (1973), in which the Court upheld the legality of a warrantless search of a disabled car; Cupp v. Murphy, 412 U.S. 291 (1973), in which it was held lawful to seize fingernail scrapings without a warrant; Schneckloth v. Bustamonte, 412 U.S. 218 (1973), in which it was held that an individual can voluntarily consent to a search without knowledge of his right to refuse.

The Court ruled against the police and prosecutors in Bivens v. Six Unknown Agents, 403 U.S. 388 (1971), in which it was held that a citizen may recover damages against the police for violation of Fourth Amendment rights; Coolidge v. New Hampshire, 403 U.S. 443 (1971), in which a warrantless search of a car was declared invalid; Whiteley v. Warden of Wyoming State Penitentiary, 401 U.S. 560 (1971), in which an arrest warrant was held invalid because not based upon probable cause; United States v. United States District Court, 407 U.S. 297 (1972), in which the warrantless electronic surveillance of domestic subversives was held illegal; Almeida-Sanchez v. United States, 413 U.S. 266 (1973), in which it was held that warrantless searches of cars within one hundred miles of the United States border were unconstitutional.

arrest whether or not weapons or evidence of the crime justifying the arrest are sought.

—A warrantless search and seizure of an automobile and warrantless search and seizure of an arrestee's clothes were constitutional.

—Consent to search the premises of an accused may be obtained from a third party with common authority over the premises.

In other decisions favorable to the police and prosecutors, the Court limited the retroactive impact of *Miranda* v. *Arizona*, 384 U.S. 436 (1966), and upheld the constitutionality of tests conducted without warrants to detect violations of environmental laws. The Court also sustained the validity of forfeiture statutes that provide for the seizure, without notice, of property used in a criminal enterprise and its condemnation even if the owner is innocent of wrongdoing.

Of the three wiretap cases decided this term, two were especially notable. In one case, the Court invalidated hundreds of prosecutions on the ground that the federal wiretap laws require that applications for a court-authorized wiretap be made by the attorney general or a specially designated assistant attorney general. The wiretaps in question had been applied for by the attorney general's executive assistant, who lacked the necessary authority. In a companion case, the Court ruled that evidence from a court-authorized wiretap need not be suppressed merely because the application for the tap misidentified the person authorizing the application in violation of federal law.

United States v. Calandra, 414 U.S. 338 (1974)

Facts: A grand jury witness refused to answer certain questions on the ground that they were based on evidence obtained from an unconstitutional search and seizure in violation of the Fourth Amendment. A lower federal court upheld the claim and ordered that the witness need not answer any grand jury questions based upon evidence obtained in violation of the Fourth Amendment.

Question: May a witness refuse to answer grand jury questions based upon evidence seized in violation of the Fourth Amendment?

Decision: No. Opinion by Justice Powell. Vote: 6–3, Brennan, Douglas, and Marshall dissenting.

Reasons: In *Weeks* v. *United States*, 232 U.S. 383 (1914), and *Mapp* v. *Ohio*, 367 U.S. 643 (1961), the Supreme Court held that evidence obtained in violation of the Fourth Amendment's prohibition of unreasonable searches and seizures could not be used in a criminal proceeding against the victim of that violation (the exclusionary rule). Although its purpose is to deter police from violating the Fourth Amendment, "the exclusionary rule has never been interpreted to proscribe the use of illegally-seized evidence in all proceedings or against all persons." The Supreme Court has ruled, for example, that evidence seized illegally may be introduced in criminal trials against persons who were not victims of that illegality. Thus, to determine whether the exclusionary rule should apply to grand jury proceedings the "potential injury to the historic role and functions of the grand jury [must be weighed] against the potential benefits of the rule as applied in this context." The additional deterrent effect against Fourth Amendment violations achieved by extending the exclusionary rule to grand jury proceedings "is uncertain at best." On the other hand, the Court noted that "[p]ermitting witnesses to invoke the exclusionary rule before a grand jury would precipitate adjudication of issues hitherto reserved for trial on the merits and would delay and disrupt grand jury proceedings." A balancing of the relevant interests involved compels the conclusion that the exclusionary rule should not apply in grand jury proceedings.

The Court also rejected the contention that each grand jury question based upon evidence obtained in violation of the Fourth Amendment constitutes a new Fourth Amendment violation and thus should be suppressed.

United States v. Robinson, 414 U.S. 218 (1973)

Facts: The defendant, under custodial arrest for operating a motor vehicle after revocation of his operator's permit, was subjected to a full police search that uncovered a cigarette package containing heroin. At his trial for illegal possession of heroin, the defendant unsuccessfully moved to suppress the evidence of heroin discovered by the police search. He claimed that the search violated the Fourth Amendment's prohibition of unreasonable searches. The police conceded that the challenged search was conducted neither to remove weapons nor to discover evidence of the crime for which the defendant was arrested.

Question: Does the Fourth Amendment permit a full police search after custodial arrest irrespective of whether weapons or evidence of the crime justifying the arrest are sought?

Decision: Yes. Opinion by Justice Rehnquist. Vote: 6–3, Marshall, Douglas, and Brennan dissenting.

Reasons: Several prior Supreme Court opinions have affirmed in dicta the existence of an unqualified authority to search incident to a lawful arrest. The principles of stare decisis do not prevent a reexamination of those dicta. However, reexamination produces no evidence that the framers of the Fourth Amendment intended to prohibit full searches incident to custodial arrests unless weapons or evidence of the crime justifying the arrest were sought reasonably: "A police officer's determination as to how and where to search the person of a suspect whom he has arrested is necessarily a quick *ad hoc* judgment which the Fourth Amendment does not require to be broken down in each instance into an analysis of each step in the search. . . . It is the fact of the lawful arrest which establishes the authority to search. . . ."

Cardwell v. *Lewis*, 417 U.S. 583 (1974)

Facts: Lewis was granted habeas corpus relief on the ground that evidence obtained from the warrantless seizure of his automobile and the examination of its exterior was used at his trial in violation of the Fourth Amendment. The automobile was seized from a public commercial parking lot and towed to a police impoundment lot after Lewis was arrested. The day after its seizure, the car's exterior was examined without a warrant. The examination revealed that a tire matched the cast of a tire impression made at the crime scene and that paint samples taken from the car matched the paint on the fender of the victim's car. That evidence was introduced at Lewis' trial for first-degree murder.

Question: Did either the warrantless seizure of the automobile or the warrantless examination of its exterior violate the Fourth Amendment's prohibition against unreasonable searches and seizures?

Decision: No. Opinion by Justice Blackmun. Vote: 5–4, Stewart, Douglas, Brennan, and Marshall dissenting.

Reasons: The primary object of the Fourth Amendment is to shield the citizen from unwarranted intrusions into his privacy. One has a lesser expectation of privacy in a motor vehicle than in a home "because its function is transportation and it seldom serves as one's residence or as the repository of personal effects." Moreover, in this case the challenged "search" of the car was "limited to the examination of the tire on the wheel and the taking of paint scrapings from the exterior. . . ." In such circumstances, the search did not infringe upon any expectation of privacy; thus no warrant was needed for its justification. Since it is conceded that the police had probable cause to search the car, the examination of its exterior did not violate the Fourth Amendment.

The warrantless seizure of the car from a public parking lot was also reasonable under the Fourth Amendment. Probable cause for the seizure is conceded. The failure to secure a warrant was justified to prevent removal of the car, which could have led to destruction of incriminating evidence. It was argued that probable cause to search the car existed long before its seizure and thus no "exigent circumstances" justified the police action without a warrant. "Assuming that probable cause previously existed, we know of no case or principle that suggests that the right to search on probable cause and the reasonableness of seizing a car under exigent circumstances are foreclosed if a warrant was not obtained at the first practicable moment."

United States v. *Edwards*, 415 U.S. 800 (1974)

Facts: The morning after his arrest and jailing, Edwards' clothes were seized by the police and searched without a warrant. The search, conducted with probable cause, revealed evidence (paint chips) linking Edwards to the crime for which he was charged. At his trial, Edwards moved to exclude the paint chips and clothes as evidence on the ground that the warrantless search and seizure of his clothing violated the Fourth Amendment prohibition against unreasonable searches. Reversing the district court's decision denying the motion, the court of appeals held that although probable cause existed to believe that evidence of crime would be discovered by the search, the warrantless seizure of the clothing carried out "after the administrative process and mechanics of arrest have come to a halt" violated the Fourth Amendment.

Question: Did the warrantless seizure of Edwards' clothing shortly after his arrest and incarceration violate the Fourth Amendment?

Decision: No. Opinion by Justice White. Vote: 5–4, Stewart, Douglas, Brennan, and Marshall dissenting.

Reasons: Once Edwards was incarcerated, the police were entitled to seize his clothes with or without probable cause. The short delay in so doing in this case was justified because no substitute clothes were available for Edwards to wear on the night he was jailed.

> When it became apparent [the following morning] that the articles of clothing were evidence of the crime for which Edwards was being held, the police were entitled to take, examine, and preserve them for use as evidence, just as they are normally permitted to seize evidence of crime when it is lawfully encountered. . . . [I]t is difficult to perceive what is unreasonable about the police examining and holding as evidence those personal effects of the accused that they al-

ready have in their lawful custody as the result of a lawful arrest.

United States v. Matlock, 415 U.S. 164 (1974)

Facts: At his trial for robbery, the defendant moved to suppress evidence seized without a search warrant by law enforcement officers from a home in which he had been living. The challenged evidence was seized in a bedroom after a third party, Mrs. Graff, who said she jointly occupied the bedroom with Matlock, voluntarily consented to the search. Matlock contended that Mrs. Graff had no authority to consent to a search of his bedroom and thus the evidence was seized in violation of the Fourth Amendment's prohibition against unreasonable searches. The district court granted the motion to suppress, holding that where consent by a third person is relied upon as justification for a search under the Fourth Amendment, the government must show that the person had actual authority to consent; a reasonable belief that such authority existed was held insufficient. Additionally, the district court ruled that certain out-of-court statements made by Mrs. Graff were inadmissable as evidence to prove her actual authority to consent to the search because they were hearsay.

Questions: (1) Did the district court err in ruling that Mrs. Graff had insufficient authority to consent to the challenged authority? (2) Should the statements made by Mrs. Graff have been admitted into evidence?

Decision: Yes to both questions. Opinion by Justice White. Vote: 6–3, Douglas, Brennan, and Marshall dissenting.

Reasons: Past cases establish the proposition that "when the prosecution seeks to justify a warrantless search by proof of voluntary consent, it is not limited to proof that the consent was given by the defendant, but may show that permission to search was obtained from a third party who possessed common authority over or other sufficient relationship to the premises or effects sought to be inspected." Mrs. Graff's out-of-court statements, tending to show that she and Matlock were husband and wife and jointly shared the searched bedroom, seemed to establish that she possessed sufficient common authority over control of the bedroom to validate her consent to the search. The district court should have admitted Mrs. Graff's out-of-court statements to prove "common authority" because they had the indicia of trustworthiness. Even assuming such statements might be characterized as hearsay, they should not have been excluded for that reason alone, because "the rules of evidence normally applicable in criminal

19

trials do not operate with full force at hearings before the judge to determine the admissibility of evidence." Stating its belief that the evidence established Mrs. Graff's consent to the search, the Court nevertheless ordered the case returned to the district court for further proceedings consistent with its opinion.

Air Pollution Variance Board of Colorado v. Western Alfalfa Corp., 416 U.S. 861 (1974)

Facts: Without a warrant, a state health inspector entered a company's outdoor premises to make an opacity test of smoke being emitted from its chimneys. The results of the test were used in connection with an administrative hearing in which it was determined that the chimney emissions violated state environmental laws. The company unsuccessfully contended that the warrantless opacity test was made in violation of its Fourth Amendment right against unreasonable searches and thus the test results should have been suppressed.

Question: Was the opacity test made in violation of the Fourth Amendment?

Decision: No. Opinion by Justice Douglas. Vote: 9–0.

Reasons: In *Hester* v. *United States*, 265 U.S. 52 (1924), the Court held that the Fourth Amendment does not offer protection to sights seen in "the open fields." In this case, the state health inspector sighted the chimney emissions in the sky. He made his challenged opacity test on company premises from which the public was not excluded. Any consequent invasion of privacy that the company may have suffered is "abstract and theoretical." Accordingly, the state health inspector was operating "well within the 'open fields' exception to the Fourth Amendment approved in *Hester*" in making the opacity test without a warrant.

Michigan v. Tucker, 417 U.S. 433 (1974)

Facts: Under interrogation while in custody as a suspected rapist, Tucker disclosed the identity of a witness who subsequently testified against Tucker in his state court trial. Before the questioning commenced, Tucker was informed of his right to remain silent and his right to counsel. He was not told that counsel would be appointed for him if he was indigent. The questioning occurred before the Supreme Court's landmark decision in *Miranda* v. *Arizona*, 384 U.S. 436 (1966). There the Court held that "the prosecution may not use statements, whether exculpatory or inculpatory, stemming from custodial interrogation of the defendant unless it demonstrates the use of procedural safeguards effective to secure the privilege against self-incrimination." The Court added that if the following procedures were followed, statements made by a suspect would not violate his Fifth Amendment privilege against compulsory self-incrimination: "Prior to any questioning, the person must be warned that he has a right to remain silent, that any statement he does make may be used as evidence against him, and that he has a right to the presence of an attorney, either retained or appointed."

Tucker's trial, at which he was convicted, occurred after *Miranda*. *Johnson* v. *New Jersey*, 384 U.S. 719 (1966), held that *Miranda* applied to trials occurring after the date it was decided and thus applied to Tucker's trial.

Tucker sought habeas corpus relief in federal district court on the ground that the trial judge erred in refusing to suppress the testimony of the witness he had identified during police interrogation without having received the full *Miranda* warnings. The district court granted the relief on the theory that the privilege against self-incrimination required the suppression of all evidence derived solely from statements made by Tucker without full *Miranda* warnings.

Question: Did the trial court's refusal to suppress the testimony of the witness Tucker identified during police interrogation violate the Fifth Amendment or other constitutional provisions and thus entitle him to habeas corpus relief?

Decision: No. Opinion by Justice Rehnquist. Vote: 8–1, Douglas dissenting.

Reasons: The constitutional privilege against compulsory self-incrimination protects a defendant only against the use of statements that are "involuntarily" made or legally coerced. Tucker's interrogation by the police "involved no compulsion sufficient to breach the right against self-incrimination" but only constituted a disregard of the procedural safeguards associated with that right since *Miranda*. Accordingly, the question raised in this case is whether this disregard should require the suppression of the testimony of the witness who was identified during the police questioning.

The primary reason for excluding evidence derived from Fourth or Fifth Amendment violations is the deterrence of future misconduct. To have excluded the challenged testimony in this case because the police failed to give Tucker full *Miranda* warnings would not have served this purpose because the failure occurred before *Miranda*. A second reason for the exclusionary rule is protection of the courts from reliance on untrustworthy evidence. That reason has no application in this case, because the challenged testimony "was subject to the normal testing process of an adversary trial." An additional reason urged for excluding the challenged testimony is that our adversary system of justice requires the government to shoulder the entire burden of proving an individual guilty. However, a defendant may be required under the Constitution to give physical evidence against himself, and statements made by a defendant after having received full *Miranda* warnings may be used against him. In the circumstances of this case, the use of Tucker's statements to identify a witness whose testimony is used at trial "does no violence to such elements of the adversarial system as may be embodied in the Fifth, Sixth, and Fourteenth Amendments."

Calero-Toledo v. *Pearson Yacht Leasing Co.*, 416 U.S. 663 (1974)

Facts: Puerto Rican statutes provide for the seizure and forfeiture of vessels used for unlawful purposes without prior notice and without a prior adversary hearing. Pursuant to these statutes, a pleasure yacht was seized because it had been used by the lessee of the yacht to transport marijuana in violation of Puerto Rican narcotics laws. The lessor of the yacht was not involved in the lessee's criminal enterprise and had no knowledge that his vessel was being used in connection with a violation of Puerto Rican law. After seizure, the lessor filed suit seeking a declaration that the Puerto Rican forfeiture statutes had (1) denied him due process of law insofar as they authorized Puerto Rican authorities to seize the yacht without notice or a prior adversary hearing, and (2) unconstitutionally deprived him of property without just compensation.

Question: Was application of the Puerto Rican forfeiture statutes to the lessor unconstitutional in any respect?

Decision: No. Opinion by Justice Brennan. Vote: 7–2. Stewart joined the majority opinion with regard to the question of whether application of the forfeiture statutes deprived the lessor of property without just compensation. Douglas and Stewart dissented with regard to the due process question.

Reasons: Fuentes v. *Shevin*, 407 U.S. 67 (1972), reaffirmed the principle that "in limited circumstances, immediate seizure of a property interest, without an opportunity for prior hearing, is constitutionally permissible." Such circumstances are met when (1) the seizure is necessary to protect an important public interest, (2) there is a special need for speedy action, and (3) the person initiating the seizure is a government official acting under the standards of a narrowly drawn statute. These three circumstances were present in this case. The challenged seizure served the important public interest "in preventing continued illicit use of the property and in enforcing criminal sanctions." Preseizure notice and hearing might have permitted the yacht to be removed to another jurisdiction, destroyed, or concealed. And the seizure was initiated by Puerto Rican officials pursuant to Puerto Rican statutes. Accordingly, "this case presents an 'extraordinary' situation in which postponement of notice and hearing until after seizure did not deny due process."

The claim that forfeiture statutes authorize the government to seize and use the property of innocent parties without making just compensation is also meritless. Federal and state forfeiture statutes have existed since the adoption of the Constitution and have an earlier history in the colonies and in England. Supreme Court decisions have repeatedly upheld the constitutionality of forfeiture statutes as applied to innocent owners.

> [T]he Puerto Rican forfeiture statutes further the punitive and deterrent purposes that have been found sufficient to uphold, against constitutional challenge, the application of other forfeiture statutes to the property of innocents. Forfeiture of conveyances that have been used—and may be used again —in violation of the narcotics laws fosters the purposes served by the underlying criminal statutes, both by preventing further illicit use of the conveyance and by imposing an economic penalty, thereby rendering illegal behavior unprofitable. . . . To the extent that such forfeiture provisions are applied to lessors, bailors, or secured creditors who are innocent of any wrongdoing, confiscation may have the desirable effect of inducing them to exercise greater care in transferring possession of their property.

The Court warned, however, that application of forfeiture statutes when they would not serve to prevent illicit use of the property in question would raise serious constitutional questions. The Court concluded that with regard to an "owner who proved not only that he was uninvolved in and unaware of the wrongful activity, but also that he had done all that reasonably could be expected to prevent the proscribed use of his property . . . it would be difficult to conclude that forfeiture served legitimate purposes and was not unduly oppressive."

United States v. Giordano, 416 U.S. 505 (1974)

Facts: Title III of the Omnibus Crime Control and Safe Streets Act of 1968, 18 U.S. Code 2510–2520, prescribes the procedure for securing judicial authority to intercept wire communications. Section

2516(1) of 18 U.S. Code provides that the "Attorney General or any Assistant Attorney General specially designated by the Attorney General may authorize an application to a Federal judge . . . for . . . an order authorizing or approving the interception of wire or oral communications by" federal investigative agencies seeking evidence of certain designated offenses. Sections 2515 and 2518(10)(a)(i) of 18 U.S. Code provide that communications "unlawfully intercepted" under the act may be suppressed in federal criminal proceedings. Accused of violating federal narcotics laws, Giordano moved to suppress the results of court-authorized interceptions of communications on his telephone on the ground that the executive assistant of the attorney general had applied for the court-authorized wiretap. He contended that section 2516(1) permitted only the attorney general or a specially designated assistant attorney general to make such applications. Therefore, he reasoned, the challenged communications and any derivative evidence were "unlawfully intercepted" within the meaning of section 2518(10)(a)(i) and thus should be suppressed.

Question: Must the intercepted communications and the evidence derived therefrom be suppressed under the Omnibus Crime Control Act?

Decision: Yes. Opinion by Justice White. Vote: 9–0, Burger, Powell, Blackmun, and Rehnquist dissenting in part regarding the question of whether certain evidence was derived from the unlawfully intercepted communications.

Reasons: On its face, section 2516(1) does not authorize the executive assistant for the attorney general to apply for intercept authority. "The mature judgment of a particular, responsible Department of Justice official is interposed as a critical condition to any judicial order." Accordingly, the mandate of section 2516(1) was violated when the court authorized the interception of the challenged communications upon the application of the executive assistant. The legislative history of that section supports this conclusion. The clear purpose of section 2516(1) was to centralize the formulation of law enforcement policy on the use of electronic surveillance techniques in a high-ranking official responsible to the public and subject to the political process.

The challenged communications must therefore be suppressed under section 2518(10)(a)(i), because they were "unlawfully intercepted" under the act in question. The government contends that paragraph (i) was intended only to reach constitutional and not statutory violations and thus suppression is not required. However, "[t]he words 'unlawfully intercepted' are themselves not limited to constitutional violations, and we think Congress intended to require suppression where there is failure to satisfy any of those statutory requirements that directly and substantially implement the congressional intention to limit the use of intercept procedures to those situations clearly calling for the employment of this extraordinary investigative device." The provision limiting the authority to apply for court-authorized interception of communications to the attorney general or a specifically designated assistant attorney general plays a "central role in the statutory scheme and . . . suppression must follow when it is shown that this statutory requirement has been ignored."

The Court then faced the question of whether communications intercepted pursuant to a court order authorizing an extension of the initial improperly authorized order must be suppressed. Under section 2518, an extension order is proper only if the results of the initial order are shown to the court, and if the court makes the same findings that are required in connection with the original order. Those findings include (1) probable cause in the traditional sense, (2) proof that normal investigative procedures are unlikely to succeed, and (3) "probable cause for believing that particular communications concerning the offense will be obtained through the interception and for believing that the facilities or place from which the wire or oral communications are to be intercepted . . . will be used in connection with the commission of such offense or are under lease to the suspect or commonly used by him." The Court concluded that the communications invalidly intercepted pursuant to the initial order were used as important evidence to justify the findings upon which the extension order was based. Additionally, the requirement that the results of the initial order be placed before the Court as a condition to receiving an extension order was met only by disclosing the illegally intercepted communications. The Court thus held that "the results of the conversations overheard under the initial order were essential, both in fact and in law, to any extension of the intercept authority . . . [and thus] communications intercepted under the extension order are derivative evidence and must be suppressed."

The Court also concluded that evidence obtained from a pen register device should be suppressed because derived from the initial invalid intercept order. (A pen register device records on paper tape all numbers dialed from a certain telephone line but does not identify the telephone numbers from which incoming calls originated.)

United States v. Chavez, 416 U.S. 562 (1974)

Facts: Title III of the Omnibus Crime Control and Safe Streets Act of 1968, 18 U.S. Code, 2510–2520, establishes procedures for obtaining court orders authorizing the interception of a wire or oral communication. [See *United States* v. *Giordano*, 416 U.S. 505 (1974)]. Section 2516(1) limits the federal officials who may authorize an application for a court order authorizing interceptions to the attorney general or to an assistant attorney general specially designated by the attorney general. Section 2518(1)(a) requires each wiretap application to state, *inter alia*, the identity of the officer approving the application. Similarly, section 2518(4)(d) requires a court order approving a wiretap to specify the identity of the person authorizing the application. A defendant charged with federal narcotics violations moved to suppress the results of a court-authorized wiretap on the ground that the application for the court order and the order itself misidentified the official authorizing the application. The application and order incorrectly identified an assistant attorney general rather than the attorney general as the authorizing officer. The defendant contended that the intercepted communications should be suppressed under sections 2518(10)(a)(i) and (ii) that require suppression if a communication was "unlawfully intercepted" under the act or if "the order of authorization or approval under which it was intercepted is insufficient on its face."

Question: Must the intercepted communications be suppressed under paragraph (i) or (ii) of section 2518(10)(a)?

Decision: No. Opinion by Justice White. Vote: 5–4, Douglas, Brennan, Stewart, and Marshall dissenting.

Reasons: Clearly, the application and order for the challenged wiretap incorrectly identified the official authorizing the application in violation of sections 2518(1)(a) and (4)(d). This defect did not render the order constitutionally invalid. Accordingly, suppression of the intercepted communications is required only if Congress has so mandated under the act.

United States v. *Giordano* held that a communication was "unlawfully intercepted" within the meaning of section 2518(10)(a)(i) and thus must be suppressed if it was obtained in violation "of those statutory requirements that directly and substantially implement the congressional intention to limit the use of intercept procedures to those situations clearly calling for the employment of this extraordinary investigative device." The purpose of the identification requirements in sections 2518(1)(a) and (4)(d) was "to make clear who bore the responsibility for approval of the submission of a particular wiretap application." Although compliance with these sections "can simplify the assurance that those who Title III makes responsible for determining when and how wiretapping and electronic surveillance should be conducted have fulfilled their roles in each case, they do not establish a substantive role to be played in the regulatory system." Accordingly, under the reasoning of *Giordano*, violation of the identification reporting requirements does not require suppression of the resulting intercepted communications under section 2518(10)(a)(i).

With regard to paragraph (ii), the application for the wiretap and the court order were not insufficient on the surface, because they identified an assistant attorney general as the person who authorized the application to be made. "Under 2516(1), he properly could give such approval had he been specially designated to do so by the Attorney General, as the order recited. . . . In no realistic sense, therefore, can it be said that the order failed to identify an authorizing official who possessed statutory power to approve the making of the application." The Court thus concluded that suppression of the intercepted communications was not required.

United States v. Kahn, 415 U.S. 143 (1974)

Facts: A federal district judge authorized the government to wiretap the home telephones of Irving Kahn, a suspected bookmaker, and "others as yet unknown," pursuant to 18 U.S. Code, 2518. The government, in the course of intercepting conversations pursuant to the court order, overheard incriminating statements made by both Irving Kahn and his wife. Mrs. Kahn was subsequently indicted for violating the Travel Act. At trial, she moved to suppress her incriminating conversations on the ground that they were illegally intercepted under section 2518. The court of appeals reversed a district court order denying the motion. It reasoned that section 2518 excluded from the term "others as yet unknown" any persons whom further investigation would disclose were engaged in the criminal activities under investigation. Since the government had not shown that further investigation of Mrs. Kahn's activities would not have implicated her in the gambling business, she was not "a person as yet unknown" within the meaning of the wiretap order.

Question: Were Mrs. Kahn's conversations illegally intercepted under section 2518?

Decision: No. Opinion by Justice Stewart. Vote: 6–3, Douglas, Brennan, and Marshall dissenting.

Reasons: Section 2518 requires that the government, in seeking a wiretap order, state "the identity of the person, if known, *committing the offense* and whose communications are to be intercepted." This statutory language plainly requires the naming of a specific individual in a wiretap application only when law enforcement officials believe such individual to be actually committing an offense. Since Mrs. Kahn was not known by the government to be engaging in crime at the time the interception was sought, the failure to include her name in the application to wiretap Mr. Kahn's telephones was not improper. The court of appeals erroneously interpreted section 2518 as requiring a wiretap application to identify "all persons, known or discoverable, who are committing the offense and whose communications are to be intercepted." If Congress had intended a wiretap application to identify all persons whom careful investigation by the government would disclose to be engaged in the illegal activities under investigation, it would have done so with "language plainer than that now embodied in section 2518."

The Court also rejected the contention that section 2518 limited the interception of conversations only to those involving the person or persons named in the wiretap application. The Court thus ruled that the intercepted conversations to which Mr. Kahn was not a party were legally authorized under section 2518 and need not be suppressed.

Criminal Law: Rights of the Accused

The Burger Court's treatment of the rights of the accused has not been notably consistent in recent years. The Court's decisions concerning the unconstitutional vagueness of criminal statutes, the effect of a guilty plea on the waiver of constitutional rights, and the right to impose harsher penalties upon an accused after a successful appeal illustrate some inconsistency.

In *Smith* v. *Goguen*, 415 U.S. 566 (1974), the Court held that the phrase "treats contemptuously" in a state flag misuse statute was unconstitutionally vague. In contrast, later in the term the Court held in *Parker* v. *Levy*, 417 U.S. 733 (1974), that the phrases "conduct unbecoming an officer and gentleman" and "all disorders and neglects to the prejudice of good order and discipline in the armed forces" satisfied constitutional requirements of specificity. The distinguishing fact was that *Parker* concerned prohibitions placed on the conduct of military personnel. The Court reasoned that military regulations required less specificity than prohibitions applicable in civilian society.

In *Tollett* v. *Henderson*, 411 U.S. 258 (1973), the Court held that a guilty plea constitutes a waiver of a right to challenge any constitutional violations occurring prior to the plea. This term in *Blackledge* v. *Perry*, 417 U.S. 21 (1974), the Court held that a guilty plea did not constitute a waiver of the right to challenge the constitutionality of the charge to which the accused pleaded. Whether a constitutional violation occurred prior to a guilty plea or infected the charge itself, however, would seem immaterial to the question of whether a guilty plea should automatically rule out subsequent challenge to constitutional violations.

In *Chaffin* v. *Stynchcombe*, 412 U.S. 17 (1973), the Court held that states could permit a second jury to impose on a defendant whose conviction was set aside on appeal a sentence higher than that imposed by the initial jury. The Court reasoned that there was little danger that the second jury would be vindictive in its sentencing and that a defendant would thus be discouraged from exercising his right to appeal. In *North Carolina* v. *Pearce*, 395 U.S. 711 (1969), the Court held that a judge whose rulings were overturned on appeal generally could not increase the defendant's sentence after retrial, because the threat of such an increase based upon resentment might discourage the exercise of the right to appeal. This term, the Court held in *Blackledge* v. *Perry* that a prosecutor may not bring more serious charges against a defendant who has exercised his right to obtain a trial *de novo* on the initial charge. The Court reasoned that the prosecutor would probably bring a more serious charge to discourage a trial *de novo* and thereby limit his workload, but it seems equally reasonable to conclude that a prosecutor would seek to have a second jury on retrial impose a heavier sentence after a successful appeal in an effort to discourage appeals. The prosecutor's decision to seek a higher sentence would have a substantial impact on the jury sentence, because the prosecution determines what evidence to present and argues to the jury. Thus, the different outcomes in *Chaffin* and *Blackledge* do not seem readily explicable on grounds of constitutional principle.

The Burger Court's inability to decide criminal law cases on the basis of consistent constitutional principles is certainly a reflection of the philosophical division of the justices into three groups: Douglas, Brennan, and Marshall are strong defenders of the rights of the accused; Burger, Blackmun, and Rehnquist are strong defenders of the right of the community to protect itself from criminals; Stewart, White, and Powell are not as strongly committed to either view, but they tend to give more weight to the interests of effective law enforcement than do Douglas, Brennan, and Marshall.

Generally speaking, the Burger Court this term was somewhat more hospitable to the claims of defendants than it has been in previous terms, as reflected in the following rulings:

—Public contractors cannot be penalized for refusing to waive their Fifth Amendment privilege against self-incrimination.

—An accused may not be denied the right to discredit an adverse witness in order to protect the anonymity of juvenile offenders.

—An accused has a right to a jury trial in contempt proceedings if he receives a cumulative sentence exceeding six months' imprisonment.

—An accused has a right to notice of the charges and an opportunity to respond in contempt proceedings.

—A 1972 decision holding that an indigent has a right to counsel in any criminal case that may result in imprisonment is to be accorded retroactive effect.

The Court, however, departed from a series of rulings extending the right of indigents to counsel by holding that no right to counsel exists when discretionary review of criminal convictions is sought. The Court also ruled that an indigent could be required to reimburse the state for attorneys' fees paid in his defense as a condition of probation.

In a case concerning the Fifth Amendment protection against compulsory self-incrimination, the Court ruled that the privilege may not be invoked to protect documents or records held in a "representative" rather than in a "personal" capacity.

Smith v. Goguen, 415 U.S. 566 (1974)

Facts: For wearing a four-by-six-inch cloth version of the United States flag on the seat of his trousers, Goguen was convicted of violating a Massachusetts flag misuse statute. Goguen was convicted under that part of the statute which imposes criminal liability upon whomever "treats contemptuously" the flag of the United States. Goguen was subsequently granted habeas corpus relief by a lower federal court on the ground, *inter alia*, that the phrase "treats contemptuously" in the Massachusetts statute was unconstitutionally vague under the due process clause of the Fourteenth Amendment.

Question: Is the phrase "treats contemptuously" in the Massachusetts flag misuse statute unconstitutionally vague?

Decision: Yes. Opinion by Justice Powell. Vote: 6–3, Blackmun, Burger, and Rehnquist dissenting.

Reasons: The constitutional due process doctrine of vagueness, together with the corresponding requirement that criminal statutes be reasonably specific, serves several purposes. First, it guarantees every person fair warning of what is prohibited. Second, it assures reasonably clear guidelines to courts and law enforcement officials to prevent arbitrary and discriminatory enforcement of the statute. Third, it prevents a "chilling effect" on the exercise of constitutionally protected activity under the First Amendment in cases where a statute prohibits speech or conduct falling outside the protection of the First Amendment.

In this case, the phrase "treats contemptuously" has two earmarks of an unconstitutionally vague criminal statute. It fails to give fair notice of what type of treatment of the United States flag was prohibited. "[I]n a time of widely varying attitudes and tastes for displaying something as ubiquitous as the United States flag or representations of it, it could hardly be the purpose of the Massachusetts Legislature to make criminal every informal use of the flag. The statutory language under which Goguen was charged, however, fails to draw reasonably clear lines between the kinds of nonceremonial treatment that are criminal and those that are not." Additionally, the phrase in question is sufficiently unbounded to prohibit any public deviation from formal flag etiquettes. "Statutory language of such a standardless sweep allows policemen, prosecutors, and juries to pursue their personal predilections. . . . Where inherently vague statutory language permits such selective law enforcement, there is a denial of due process."

Parker v. *Levy*, 417 U.S. 733 (1974)

Facts: Article 133 of the Uniform Code of Military Justice provides for punishment of a commissioned officer for "conduct unbecoming an officer and gentleman." Article 134 of the code provides for punishment of military personnel for, *inter alia*, "all disorders and neglects to the prejudice of good order and discipline in the armed forces." An Army physician (Levy) was convicted by a general court-martial of violating Articles 133 and 134 for publicly urging Negro enlisted men to disobey orders to go to Vietnam or to fight there, and characterizing Special Forces personnel as "liars and thieves," "killers of peasants," and "murderers of women and children." Seeking habeas corpus relief in federal district court, Levy claimed that Articles 133 and 134 were unconstitutionally vague in violation of due process and the First Amendment's guarantee of free expression.

Question: Are Articles 133 and 134 of the Uniform Code of Military Justice unconstitutionally vague?

Decision: No. Opinion by Justice Rehnquist. Vote: 5–3, Douglas, Stewart, and Brennan dissenting. Marshall did not participate.

Reasons: The Court has long recognized that military law may be shaped "to maintain the discipline essential [for the military] to perform its mission effectively" and is not subject to the same constitutional constraints as civilian law. "Because of the factors differentiating military society from civilian society . . . the proper standard of review for a vagueness challenge to the Articles of the [Uniform Code] is the standard which applies to criminal statutes regulating economic affairs." That standard prohibits punishment "where one could not reasonably understand that his contemplated conduct is proscribed."

Articles 133 and 134 of the code have a long history of judicial interpretation which have "narrowed the very broad reach of the literal language of the Articles, and at the same time . . . supplied considerable specificity by way of examples of the conduct which they cover." Although the articles still contain sizeable areas of vagueness, the conduct for which Levy was convicted was clearly within their prohibitions as indicated both in case law and in the military's Manual for Courts-Martial. "Since [Levy] could have had no reasonable doubt that his published statements urging Negro enlisted men not to go to Vietnam if ordered to do so was both 'unbecoming an officer and a gentleman,' and 'to the prejudice of good order and discipline in the armed forces,' in violation of the provisions of Article 133 and Article 134, respectively, his challenge to them as unconstitutionally vague under the Due Process Clause of the Fifth Amendment must fail."

The Court also rejected the claim that Articles 133 and 134 were unconstitutional on their face because they could be applied to proscribe speech protected by the First Amendment. The reason for permitting such constitutional attacks by one whose conduct was clearly prohibited is based upon the overriding community interest in all constitutionally protected expression. That reason "must be accorded a good deal less weight in the military [as opposed to the civilian] context." Accordingly, the Court reasoned that "[t]here is a wide range of the conduct of military personnel to which the Arts. 133 and 134 may be applied without infringement of the First Amendment. . . . [T]here may lurk at the fringes of the Articles, even in the light of their narrowing construction by the United States Court of Military Appeals, some possibility that conduct which would be ultimately held to be protected by First Amendment could be included within their prohibition. . . ." However, Articles 133 and 134 may be constitutionally applied in a sufficiently large number of cases to "preclude their invalidation for overbreadth "

Blackledge v. Perry, 417 U.S. 21 (1974)

Facts: Convicted in a North Carolina state court of the misdemeanor of assault with a deadly weapon and sentenced to six months of imprisonment, Perry exercised his absolute right to a trial *de novo* in a higher state court. (Under North Carolina law, when a trial *de novo* is requested, the prior conviction is annulled.) Prior to the trial *de novo*, the prosecutor obtained a grand jury indictment charging Perry with a felony for the same conduct that lead to his misdemeanor conviction. Perry pled guilty to the felony charge and was sentenced to five to seven years' imprisonment. Several months later Perry was granted habeas corpus relief by a federal district court on the ground that bringing the felony charge violated the double jeopardy clause of the Fifth Amendment, made applicable to the states through the Fourteenth Amendment in *Benton* v. *Maryland*, 395 U.S. 784 (1969). The district court further held that Perry had not waived his right to raise the double jeopardy claim by virtue of his guilty plea.

Question: Did the federal district court properly grant Perry habeas corpus relief?

Decision: Yes. Opinion by Justice Stewart. Vote: 7–2, Rehnquist and Powell dissenting.

Reasons: In *North Carolina* v. *Pearce*, 395 U.S. 711 (1969), the Court held that following a successful appeal and reconviction, a criminal defendant could not constitutionally receive a greater punishment than that imposed at the first trial, unless the sentencing judge made certain findings on the record. In *Pearce*, the Court reasoned that due process was offended if vindictiveness against a defendant for having successfully attacked his first conviction played a part in receiving a harsher sentence upon retrial. The lesson of *Pearce* and subsequent cases is that due process is offended by the "realistic likelihood" that vindictiveness will play a part in the imposition of a sentence following retrial after appeal. Under North Carolina law,

> [a] prosecutor clearly has a considerable stake in discouraging convicted misdemeanants from appealing and thus obtaining a trial *de novo* . . . since such an appeal will clearly require increased expenditures of prosecutorial resources before the defendant's conviction becomes final, and may even result in a formerly convicted defendant going free. And, if the prosecutor has the means readily at hand to discourage such appeals—by "upping the ante" through a felony indictment whenever a convicted misdemeanant pursues his statutory appellate remedy—the State can insure that only the most hardy defendants will brave the hazards of a *de novo* trial.

Unlike *Pearce*, in this case the prosecutor and not the judge may be vindictive in exercising power following appeal. The rationale of *Pearce*, however, was that fear of vindictiveness would deter a defendant's exercise of the right to appeal. That rationale compels the conclusion that it was "not constitutionally permissible for the State to respond to Perry's invocation of his statutory right to appeal by bringing a more serious charge against him at the trial *de novo*."

Perry's guilty plea did not constitute a waiver of his constitutional claim. North Carolina contends that *Tollett* v. *Henderson*, 411 U.S. 258 (1973), mandates a contrary conclusion. There the Court concluded that a guilty plea forecloses raising constitutional claims stemming from events occurring prior to the entry of the plea. In this case, in contrast, the constitutional claim asserted and sustained is that the very initiation of the proceedings on the felony charge operated to deny Perry due process. Perry's constitutional claim thus does not arise from events occurring prior to his plea; accordingly, *Tollett* does not govern this case.

Lefkowitz v. Turley, 414 U.S. 70 (1973)

Facts: A three-judge federal district court held unconstitutional New York statutes that penalized public contractors who refused to waive their Fifth Amendment rights against self-incrimination in answering questions concerning their contracts or other transactions. The statutes penalized the contractors by (1) cancelling their existing contracts, and (2) disqualifying them from holding further contracts with the state for certain periods. The court ruled that those statutes violated the Fifth Amendment privilege against compelled self-incrimination.

Question: Do the challenged New York statutes violate the Fifth Amendment protection against compulsory self-incrimination?

Decision: Yes. Opinion by Justice White. Vote: 9–0.

Reasons: The Fifth Amendment protects an individual from being involuntarily called as a witness against himself in any proceedings, civil or criminal, formal or informal, where the answers might incriminate him in future criminal proceedings. An individual does not forfeit this constitutional right by accepting employment with the state. Prior Supreme Court decisions unmistakably establish that a public official may not be discharged for failing to waive his Fifth Amendment rights in connection with an inquiry into his performance in office. That rule applies equally to independent contractors. "We fail to see a difference of constitutional magnitude between the threat of job loss to an employee of the State, and a threat of loss of contracts to a contractor. . . ."

The Court observed, however, that a state which had granted appropriate immunity from the use of any compelled incriminating testimony in a criminal proceeding could require contractors to answer relevant inquiries concerning the performance of their contracts or suffer the disqualifications imposed by the challenged New York statutes.

Davis v. Alaska, 415 U.S. 308 (1974)

Facts: On trial in Alaska state court for grand larceny and burglary, the defendant (Davis) attempted to discredit the testimony of a crucial prosecution witness (Green) by revealing that he was on probation by order of a juvenile court. The purpose of such revelation was to show that Green's testimony was a product of fear or of concern for possible jeopardy to his probation and was thus untrustworthy. The trial court ruled, as required by a state provision protecting the anonymity of juvenile offenders, that Davis could not question Green as to his juvenile delinquency adjudication. Davis contended that the trial court's ruling deprived him of his right to confront witnesses against him under the Sixth and Fourteenth Amendments.

Question: Did the trial court's refusal to permit questioning of Green as to his juvenile delinquency adjudication deprive Davis of his constitutional right to confront witnesses against him?

Decision: Yes. Opinion by Chief Justice Burger. Vote: 7–2, White and Rehnquist dissenting.

Reasons: The Sixth Amendment guarantees the right of an accused in a criminal prosecution "to be confronted with the witnesses against him." This right applies to both federal and state criminal proceedings under *Pointer* v. *Texas*, 380 U.S. 400 (1965). The right of confrontation under the Sixth Amendment includes the right of cross-examination, in addition to the right to confront a witness physically. Here, Davis was denied the right of effective cross-examination of Green by the order prohibiting the revelation that Green had been adjudicated a juvenile delinquent. While recognizing the state's policy interest in protecting the confidentiality of a juvenile offender's record, the Court nevertheless concluded that such interest must yield to the vital constitutional right of an accused to cross-examine an adverse witness for bias.

Taylor v. Hayes, 418 U.S. 488 (1974)

Facts: During a turbulent state murder trial, the trial judge informed the attorney for the accused that he was in contempt of court. After the trial ended, the trial judge found the attorney guilty on eight counts of contempt without affording him an opportunity to respond to the charges. The attorney was sentenced to six months' imprisonment on each count, which a state appeals court held should be served concurrently (thereby making the sentence actually imposed six months in jail). The attorney unsuccessfully claimed before the appeals court that his conviction was unconstitutional on the following three grounds: (1) under the Sixth Amendment he was entitled to a jury trial, (2) due process guaranteed him an opportunity to respond to the contempt charges, and (3) due process required that the contempt charges be tried by a judge other than the trial judge who had become personally embroiled in controversy with the attorney.

Questions: Was the attorney constitutionally entitled to (1) a jury trial, (2) an opportunity to respond to the charges against him, or (3) trial by a judge other than the trial judge?

Decision: No to the first question and yes to the second and third questions. Opinion by Justice White. Vote: 8–1, Rehnquist dissenting.

Reasons: The Sixth Amendment guarantees a defendant a right to jury trial for "serious" as opposed to "petty" criminal offenses. The decisions of this Court have established that a contempt charge is "petty" when the "penalty actually imposed does not exceed six months or a longer penalty has not been expressly authorized by statute." Accordingly, since the attorney's actual sentence was six months' imprisonment and no statute authorized a longer sentence, he was not constitutionally entitled to a jury trial.

With regard to the attorney's asserted constitutional right to respond to the contempt charges, the Court has often reiterated that "reasonable notice of a charge and opportunity to be heard in defense before punishment" is a fundamental aspect of due process. In this case, the attorney was tried and punished after the conclusion of the murder trial. Thus the failure to afford him an opportunity to respond could not be justified by a necessity to keep order in the courtroom. Accordingly, "before an attorney is finally adjudicated in contempt and sentenced after trial for conduct during trial, he should have reasonable notice of the specific charges and opportunity to be heard in his own behalf. This is not to say, however, that a full-scale trial is appropriate. Usually, the events have occurred before the judge's own eyes, and a reporter's transcript is available. But the contemnor might at least urge, for example, that the behavior at issue was not contempt but the acceptable conduct of an attorney representing his client; or, he might present matters in mitigation or otherwise attempt to make amends with the court." Because the attorney was afforded neither notice nor an opportunity to respond to the charges against him, his conviction violated due process.

If the attorney is to be retried, due process requires that he not be tried by the trial judge. If a trial judge is the target of contemptuous conduct that "so embroil[s] him in controversy that he cannot 'hold the balance nice, clear and true between the State and the accused,' " then due process bars him from trying the contempt. In this case, the alleged contemptuous conduct engendered a sharp antagonism between the attorney and the trial judge. Accordingly, a fellow judge should have been substituted for the purpose of trying the contempt charges.

Codispoti v. *Pennsylvania*, 418 U.S. 506 (1974)

Facts: After their joint criminal trial ended, two defendants were found guilty by a judge of several charges of contemptuous conduct during the trial. The judge in the contempt proceedings imposed consecutive sentences on one defendant of six months for each of six contempts and three months for a seventh (making an aggregate sentence of over three years). The other defendant, found guilty of six separate contempts, was sentenced to five six-month terms and one two-month term, all to be served consecutively (making an aggregate sentence approximating three years). The defendants, whose demands for a jury trial on the contempt charges had been denied, appealed claiming that their Sixth Amendment rights to jury trial in criminal cases had been violated.

Question: Were the defendants denied their Sixth Amendment rights to jury trial in criminal cases?

Decision: Yes. Opinion by Justice White. Vote: 5–4, Burger, Stewart, Blackmun, and Rehnquist dissenting.

Reasons: "In *Duncan* v. *Louisiana,* 391 U.S. 145 (1968), the Court held that the Fourteenth Amendment guaranteed to defendants in state criminal trials the right to jury trial provided in the Sixth Amendment. In a companion case, *Bloom* v. *Illinois,* 391 U.S. 194 (1968), the Court held that while petty contempts, like other petty crimes, could be tried without a jury, serious criminal contempts must be tried with a jury if the defendant insisted on this mode of trial." *Bloom* and subsequent decisions have established that for purposes of the Sixth Amendment right to jury trial, crimes carrying more than a six-month sentence are serious crimes and those carrying less are petty crimes. *Bloom* also established that where sentencing is left to the entire discretion of the judge, the sentence actually imposed determines the seriousness of the crime.

In this case, contempt charges against each defendant were "tried seriatim in one proceeding, and the trial judge not only imposed [up to] a six months' sentence for each contempt but also determined that the individual sentences were to run consecutively rather than concurrently, a ruling which necessarily extended the prison term to be served beyond that allowable for a petty criminal offense. . . . In terms of the sentence imposed, which was obviously several times more than six months, each contemnor was tried for what was equivalent to a serious offense and was entitled to a jury trial."

The Court rejected the argument that the contempts "were separate offenses and that, because no more than a six months' sentence was imposed for any single offense, each contempt was necessarily a petty offense triable without a jury." The Court reasoned that the contempt charges could not realistically be separated because they "arose from a single trial, were charged by a single judge, and were tried in a single proceeding."

Berry v. City of Cincinnati, Ohio, 414 U.S. 29 (1973)

Facts: The defendant, convicted of a misdemeanor without the aid of counsel and incarcerated, unsuccessfully sought to invalidate his conviction on the ground that *Argersinger* v. *Hamlin*, 407 U.S. 25 (1972), should be accorded retroactive effect. *Argersinger* held that without a knowing and intelligent waiver, no indigent may be imprisoned for any offense unless he was represented at trial by counsel.

Question: Was the defendant's misdemeanor conviction and incarceration invalid because *Argersinger* is to be accorded retroactive effect?

Decision: Yes. Per curiam opinion. Vote: 9–0.

Reasons: "Those convicted prior to the decision in *Argersinger* are entitled to the constitutional rule enunciated in that case . . . if they allege and prove a bona fide, existing case or controversy sufficient to invoke the jurisdiction of a federal court."

Ross v. Moffitt, 417 U.S. 600 (1974)

Facts: An indigent defendant was represented by court-appointed counsel during his two North Carolina trials and convictions for forgery and on his unsuccessful appeals as of right to the state court of appeals. Thereafter, in one case he was denied appointment of counsel to prepare a petition seeking discretionary review by the North Carolina Supreme Court, and in the other case was denied appointment of counsel to prepare a petition for certiorari to the United States Supreme Court. Subsequently, the defendant was granted federal habeas corpus relief by a federal court of appeals which held that he was constitutionally entitled to the assistance of counsel at state expense both on his petition for review in the North Carolina Supreme Court and on his petition for certiorari in the United States Supreme Court. The court of appeals reasoned that the concepts of fairness and equality require that indigents have access to counsel to the same extent as wealthier persons in pursuing their rights in seeking review of criminal convictions.

Question: Is it unconstitutional for states to refuse to provide indigents with counsel when discretionary review of criminal convictions is sought?

Decision: No. Opinion by Justice Rehnquist. Vote: 6–3, Douglas, Brennan, and Marshall dissenting.

Reasons: In *Griffin v. Illinois,* 351 U.S. 12 (1956), the Court held unconstitutional an Illinois rule denying a right of appeal to a convicted criminal unless he could afford the cost of a transcript of the testimony adduced at trial. *Griffin* and subsequent cases "stand for the proposition that a State cannot arbitrarily cut off appeal rights for indigents while leaving open avenues of appeal for more affluent persons."

In *Douglas v. California,* 372 U.S. 353 (1963), the Court held that a state must provide counsel for an indigent on his first appeal as of right. The *Griffin* and *Douglas* decisions rested upon both the due process clause and the equal protection clause of the Fourteenth Amendment. Neither clause, however, requires North Carolina to provide an indigent with counsel in seeking discretionary review of a criminal conviction.

Due process is violated only if the challenged criminal procedures are fundamentally unfair to the indigent. Having had appointed counsel at both the trial and first appeal as of right, the indigent was not treated "unfairly" by North Carolina's refusal to provide him counsel at further stages of appellate review. Equal protection is denied if indigents are singled out by the state and denied meaningful access to the courts. A defendant, however, is not "denied meaningful access to the North Carolina Supreme Court simply because the State does not appoint counsel to aid him in seeking review in that court." At that stage of the proceedings, a transcript of the trial proceedings, a brief in the court of appeals setting forth claims of error (and often an opinion by that court disposing of the claims), supplemented by whatever submission a defendant might make *pro se*, "would appear to provide the Supreme Court of North Carolina with an adequate basis on which to base its decision to grant or deny review. . . . The duty of the State under our cases is not to duplicate the legal arsenal that may be privately retained by a criminal defendant in a continuing effort to reverse his conviction, but only to assure the indigent defendant an adequate opportunity to present his claims fairly in the context of the State's appellate process." Accordingly, indigent defendants have no constitutional right to appointed counsel in seeking discretionary review of their criminal convictions in the North Carolina Supreme Court.

For substantially the same reasons, the Court also concluded that the failure of a state to provide counsel for a defendant seeking review of his conviction in the United States Supreme Court by certiorari was not unconstitutional.

Fuller v. Oregon, 417 U.S. 40 (1974)

Facts: An indigent defendant, represented by court appointed counsel, pleaded guilty to a crime in Oregon state court. He was sentenced to five years of probation conditioned upon (1) compliance with a county jail work-release program permitting him to attend college, and (2) reimbursement to the county of the fees and expenses of the attorney who defended him. The defendant appealed his sentence contending that his probation, which was conditional on the reimbursement of the state-incurred attorney expenses, violated the equal protection clause of the Fourteenth Amendment and the Sixth Amendment right to counsel. The state court of appeals rejected these claims.

Question: Was the defendant's conditional probation sentence constitutional?

Decision: Yes. Opinion by Justice Stewart. Vote: 7–2, Marshall and Brennan dissenting.

Reasons: Oregon law provides that a convicted defendant's probation may be conditioned upon repayment of state-incurred attorney expenses only if several conditions are satisfied. First, the convicted person must have a real likelihood of acquiring financial resources sufficient to make the repayment. Second, the court which sentenced him may order remission of the payment at any time if payment "will impose manifest hardship on the defendant or his immediate family. . . ." Finally, no convicted person may be held in contempt for failure to repay if the failure was not willful.

The probationer argued that the Oregon statutory scheme violates equal protection, because only convicted defendants may be required to repay state-incurred attorneys' expenses. The difference in the treatment accorded convicted defendants and defendants who are not convicted under Oregon law has a rational basis and thus the equal protection claim must be denied.

> A defendant whose trial ends without conviction or whose conviction is overturned on appeal has been seriously imposed upon by society without any conclusive demonstration that he is criminally culpable. His life has been interrupted and subjected to great stress, and he may have incurred financial hardship through loss of job or potential working hours. His reputation may have been greatly damaged. . . . Oregon could surely decide with objective rationality that when a defendant has been forced to submit to a criminal prosecution that does not end in conviction, he will be freed of any potential liability to reimburse the State for the costs of his defense.

The probationer also claimed that the Oregon provisions for ordering repayment of attorneys' expenses violates the Sixth Amendment right to counsel by encouraging indigents to decline the services of an appointed attorney. However, Oregon law clearly provides counsel to an indigent at every stage of the criminal proceedings against him. Past decisions of the Supreme Court holding state laws unconstitutional for imposing a penalty upon the exercise of a constitutional right for the purpose of discouraging its exercise are inapplicable to this case. The purpose of the challenged Oregon statutes is not to chill the assertion of the constitutional right of counsel but to provide that a "convicted person who later becomes able to pay for his counsel may be required to do so."

Bellis v. United States, 417 U.S. 85 (1974)

Facts: A partner in a three-partner law firm that had been dissolved refused to comply with a grand jury subpoena to produce the firm's books and financial records on the ground that he was protected by the Fifth Amendment privilege against compulsory self-incrimination. A federal district court rejected the Fifth Amendment claim and held the partner in civil contempt.

Question: May a partner in a small law firm invoke the Fifth

Amendment to justify his refusal to comply with a subpoena requiring production of the partnership's financial records?

Decision: No. Opinion by Justice Marshall. Vote: 8–1, Douglas dissenting.

Reasons: The Court reasoned as follows:

It has long been established . . . that the Fifth Amendment privilege against compulsory self-incrimination protects an individual from compelled production of his personal papers and effects as well as compelled oral testimony. . . . [A]n equally long line of cases has established that an individual cannot rely upon the privilege to avoid producing the records of a collective entity which are in his possession in a representative capacity, even if these records might incriminate him personally. . . . The Court's decisions holding the privilege inapplicable to the records of a collective entity . . . reflect a . . . policy underlying the privilege, the protection of an individual's right to a "private enclave where he may lead a private life."

In this case, the partner held the subpoenaed partnership's records in a representative capacity, and thus the Fifth Amendment privilege could not justify his refusal to comply with the subpoena.

The partner contended that the partnership was little more than the combined personal legal practices of the individual partners and thus could not realistically be considered an independent entity distinct from the individual partners. Additionally, he argued that he did not hold the subpoenaed records in a representative capacity. Neither of these claims was supported by the facts. The partnership had no formal constitution or by-laws, but maintained a separate bank account, used special stationery, and held itself out to third parties as an independent institutional entity. The partnership was treated under state law as a distinct entity for numerous purposes. The partnership thus had an existence distinct from the individual partners. It was also clear that the partner held the subpoenaed records, the financial books and records of the partnership, in a representative capacity. Under applicable state law, all partners had a right of access to the partnership records.

"[I]n the circumstances of this case, the [partner's] possession of the partnership's financial records in what can be fairly said to be a representative capacity compels our holding that his personal privilege against compulsory self-incrimination is inapplicable." The Court noted that if records of a family partnership were involved, or if there were some other preexisting relationship of confidentiality among the partners, it might have reached a different conclusion.

Marshall v. United States, 414 U.S. 417 (1974)

Facts: With a record of three prior felonies, Marshall, a drug offender, requested at sentencing that he be considered for special treatment as a narcotic addict pursuant to Title II of the federal Narcotic Rehabilitation Act of 1966. The sentencing judge refused on the ground that under the act offenders having two or more prior felony convictions are ineligible for such special treatment and sentenced Marshall to ten years of imprisonment. Marshall sought habeas corpus relief on the ground that his sentence was illegal because the "two prior felony" exclusion rule of the act was arbitrary and unreasonable, in violation of the due process clause of the Fifth Amendment.

Question: Does the Narcotic Rehabilitation Act violate Fifth Amendment due process by preventing a sentencing judge from ordering rehabilitative commitment, in lieu of penal incarceration, for addicts with two or more prior felony convictions?

Decision: No. Opinion by Chief Justice Burger. Vote: 6–3, Douglas, Brennan, and Marshall dissenting.

Reasons: Due process requires that there be some rational basis for statutory distinctions. The purpose of the act was to provide generally for the civil commitment and treatment of narcotic addicts convicted of federal crimes, but to exclude from such treatment both those less likely to be rehabilitated and those whose records disclose a history of serious crimes. Congress could rationally have concluded that the "two prior felony rule" was justified because the criminals excluded by that rule would be less likely to respond to treatment and more likely to disrupt the sensitive environment of a drug treatment program than those with lesser criminal records. Additionally, it was rational to conclude that "an addict with multiple convictions was more 'hardened' and thus a greater potential danger to society on early release than the addict who had committed one prior felony or none."

Prisons and Prisoner Rights

Since the 1971 prison uprising at Attica, increasing attention has been given to the operations and effectiveness of prisons. Chief Justice Burger has been notable in his encouragement of prison reform and the establishment of inmate grievance procedures. The attention given to prisoner rights has led to litigation which has thrust the courts into a central role in the drive toward prison reform. Until this term, the Supreme Court had generally refrained from deciding cases concerning the day-to-day administration of prisons.[1] This term the Court decided three significant cases which generally set the constitutional parameters of prison disciplinary procedures, prisoner access to legal assistance, prisoner access to the press, and mail censorship. Generally speaking, these three decisions reflected an attitude of deference to the discretion of prison officials largely resulting from consideration of the uncertain effects of constitutionalizing a host of asserted prisoner rights. However, to characterize these decisions as an abdication to the views of prison officials would be inaccurate. The Court expanded the rights of prisoners to legal assistance, effectively nullified mail censorship regulations, and established procedural rights for prisoners in disciplinary proceedings.

The Court's three decisions established the following constitutional propositions:

—Prison regulations may prohibit press and other media interviews with specific individual inmates.

—Censorship of prisoner mail is permissible only if it furthers a substantial governmental interest unrelated to the suppression of expression and is not unnecessarily broad.

—Law students and legal paraprofessionals may not be barred from conducting inmate interviews.

—In prison disciplinary proceedings, the individual charged is entitled to notice and an opportunity to be heard. Additionally, he is entitled to call witnesses and present documentary evidence in his defense if this procedure is not hazardous to prison safety or to correctional goals. However, a prisoner has no right to confront and cross-examine his accusers.

—Prisoners must be afforded a reasonable opportunity to prepare both habeas corpus and civil rights suits.

In two other cases, the Court held that prisoners eligible to vote could not be denied the right to vote by absentee ballot, but that states could disenfranchise persons convicted of "infamous crimes."

The Court also decided a case with significance for the administration of federal habeas corpus statutes. Presently, approximately 10 percent of the civil actions filed in federal district court concern pris-

---

[1] An exception was the Court's decision in Johnson v. Avery, 393 U.S. 483 (1969). There the Court held that inmates must be permitted to furnish each other assistance in preparing habeas corpus petitions unless the state provided reasonable alternative assistance.

oner habeas corpus petitions, a dramatic rise since 1961. In an effort to decrease the judicial burden of handling habeas corpus petitions, a federal district court authorized federal magistrates under the Federal Magistrates Act to take evidence in habeas corpus cases and to recommend their disposition. The Court ruled that the act did not permit the use of magistrates to hear evidence, thus leaving with Congress the initiative to ease the impact on the federal judiciary of the large number of habeas corpus petitions.

Pell v. Procunier, 417 U.S. 817 (1974)

Facts: Four California prison inmates and three professional journalists brought suit in federal district court challenging the constitutionality of a prison regulation prohibiting "[p]ress and other media interviews with specific individual inmates. . . ." The inmates contended that the regulation violated their constitutional rights of free speech under the First Amendment. The journalists claimed that the regulation violated the freedom of the press as guaranteed by the First Amendment by limiting their newsgathering activity. The district court held that the challenged regulation unconstitutionally violated the inmates' First Amendment rights insofar as it prohibited them from having face-to-face communication with journalists. In rejecting the claims of the journalists, the district court noted that they had the freedom to enter California prisons and interview at random.

Question: Does the challenged California prison regulation violate the First Amendment rights of either inmates or journalists?

Decision: No. Opinion by Justice Stewart. Vote: 5–4 with regard to the question of whether the regulation violates the First Amendment rights of journalists and 6–3 with regard to the question of whether it violates inmates' First Amendment rights. Douglas, Brennan, and Marshall dissented. Powell joined the majority regarding the question of inmates' rights.

Reasons: "[C]hallenges to prison restrictions that are asserted to inhibit First Amendment interests must be analyzed in terms of the legitimate policies and goals of the corrections system. . . ." In this case, California permits prison inmates to communicate by mail and to receive limited visits from family members, the clergy, their attorneys, and friends. Inmates may use these channels to communicate with the press. "[S]ecurity considerations are sufficiently paramount in the administration of the prison to justify the imposition of some restrictions on the entry of outsiders into the prison for face-to-face contact with inmates." Prohibiting face-to-face interviews with the press does not violate the First Amendment rights of the California inmates in light of the alternative channels of communication that are open.

Regarding the journalists' claims, it should be noted that

> newsmen are permitted to visit both the maximum and minimum security sections of the [prisons] and to stop and speak about any subject to any inmates whom they might encounter. If security considerations permit, corrections personnel will step aside to permit such interviews to be confidential. . . . [N]ewsmen are also permitted to enter the prisons to interview inmates selected at random by the corrections officials from the prison population. . . . [I]f a newsman wishes to write a story on a particular prison program, he is permitted to sit in on group meetings and to interview the inmate participants. . . . The sole limitation on newsgathering in California prisons is the prohibition . . . of interviews with individual inmates specifically designated by representatives of the press.

The purpose of the limitation is to prevent certain inmates from acquiring excessive influence within the prison through concentrated media attention. Although this limitation hampers newsgathering, it does not restrict the press from publishing what it wishes. The claim that "the Constitution imposes upon government the affirmative duty to make available to journalists sources of information not available to members of the public generally . . . finds no support in the words of the Constitution or in any decision of this Court. Accordingly, since [the challenged regulation] does not deny the press access to sources of information available to members of the general public . . . it does not abridge the protections that the First and Fourteenth Amendments guarantee."

In a related case, *Saxbe* v. *Washington Post Co.*, 417 U.S. 843 (1974), the Court upheld the constitutionality of a Federal Bureau of Prisons provision prohibiting personal interviews between newsmen and individually designated inmates of medium and maximum security prisons. The provision was attacked by newsmen, and the Court found the case constitutionally indistinguishable from *Pell* v. *Procunier*.

Procunier v. Martinez, 416 U.S. 396 (1974)

Facts: Prison inmates brought suit in federal district court challenging the constitutionality of California prison regulations relating to censorship of prisoner mail and prohibiting law students and legal paraprofessionals from conducting attorney-client interviews with inmates. The challenged mail censorship regulations authorize prison employees to refuse to send or deliver a letter that "unduly complains," "magnifies grievances," "expresses inflammatory political, racial, religious or other views or beliefs," or contains matter deemed "defamatory" or "otherwise inappropriate." The district court held that the mail censorship regulations unconstitutionally suppressed free speech and were unconstitutionally vague. Additionally, the district court concluded that a mail censorship scheme must provide that an inmate be notified of the rejection of a letter written by or addressed to him, that the author of the letter be given a reasonable opportunity to protest that decision, and that complaints be referred to a prison official other than the person who originally disapproved the correspondence. The regulation prohibiting the use of law students and legal paraprofessionals to conduct attorney-client interviews was held unconstitutional on the ground that it restricted an inmate's right of access to the courts.

Question: Are the challenged California prison regulations unconstitutional?

Decision: Yes. Opinion by Justice Powell. Vote: 9–0.

Reasons: Prior Supreme Court decisions indicate that censorship of prisoner mail is justified only if the following criteria are met:

First, the regulation or practice in question must further an important or substantial governmental interest unrelated to the suppression of expression. Prison officials may not censor inmate correspondence simply to eliminate unflattering or unwelcome opinions or factually inaccurate statements. Rather, they must show that a regulation authorizing mail censorship furthers one or more of the substantial governmental interests of security, order, and rehabilitation. Second, the limitation of First Amendment freedoms must be no greater than is necessary or essential to the protection of the particular governmental interest involved. Thus a restriction on inmate correspondence that furthers an important or substantial interest of penal administration will nevertheless be invalid if its sweep is unnecessarily broad. This does not mean, of course, that prison administrators may be required to show with certainty that adverse consequences would flow from the failure to censor a particular letter. Some latitude in anticipating the probable consequences of allowing certain speech in a prison environment is essential to the proper discharge of an administrator's duty. But any regulation or practice that restricts inmate correspondence must be generally necessary to protect one or more of the legitimate governmental interests identified above.

Applying this standard, the challenged mail censorship regulations are unconstitutional because they were not shown to be "necessary to the furtherance of a governmental interest unrelated to the suppression of expression."

The district court also properly concluded that the interests of prisoners and their correspondents in uncensored communication constitutes "liberty" protected by the Fourteenth Amendment and thus may not be restricted unless accompanied by minimum procedural safeguards of the type it imposed.

The regulation absolutely banning the use of law students and legal paraprofessionals to conduct attorney-client interviews interferes with a lawyer's ability to adequately and efficiently represent inmates. Because not justified by any state interest, that interference unconstitutionally restricts an inmate's right of access to the courts under the principles established in *Johnson* v. *Avery*, 393 U.S. 483 (1969). The Court stated, however, that "prison administrators are not required to adopt every proposal that may . . . facilitate prisoner access to the courts." The constitutionality of regulations restricting court access should be determined by weighing the severity of the restrictions "against the legitimate interests of penal administration and the proper regard that judges should give to the expertise and discretionary authority of correctional officials."

Wolff v. *McDonnell*, 418 U.S. 539 (1974)

Facts: Inmates at a Nebraska prison filed suit in federal district court alleging that the procedures governing disciplinary proceedings violated due process, that the legal assistance provided to inmates for the preparation of habeas corpus and civil rights suits were constitutionally deficient, and that the prison regulations governing the inspection of inmates' mail to and from attorneys were unconstitutionally restrictive.

Under Nebraska law, an inmate found guilty of "flagrant or serious" misconduct may lose good-time credits (which shorten the term of confinement) or be confined in a disciplinary cell. Charges of such misconduct are investigated and appropriate discipline imposed by a three-member committee made up of prison officials. Any inmate charged with serious misconduct is provided a conference to discuss the charges with a prison supervisor and the accusing party.

A conduct report is then prepared and a hearing held before the three-member disciplinary committee. At the hearing, the report is read to the inmate, and the inmate has an opportunity to ask questions of the party making the charges. However, an inmate has no right to counsel, to cross-examination or confrontation of adverse witnesses, or to witnesses in his behalf.

The challenged regulation concerning legal assistance provided that only a legal advisor appointed by the warden could assist inmates in preparing legal documents.

The challenged regulation regarding mail to and from attorneys, having been narrowed in the course of litigation, provided that such mail could be opened in the presence of the inmate in order to search for contraband but that it could not be read by prison authorities.

Questions: Are the challenged Nebraska prison regulations governing (1) disciplinary proceedings, (2) legal assistance, and (3) the inspection of mail to and from attorneys unconstitutional?

Decision: Yes as to questions (1) and (2) and no as to question (3). Opinion by Justice White. Vote: 6–3, Douglas, Brennan, and Marshall dissenting.

Reasons: The challenged prison procedures governing disciplinary proceedings resulting in the loss of good-time credits must conform with due process. "[T]he Constitution itself does not guarantee good-time credit for satisfactory behavior while in prison." However, since the state has created the right to good time and recognized that its deprivation is a sanction authorized for major misconduct, the prisoner's interest in good-time credit has "real substance and is sufficiently embraced within Fourteenth Amendment 'liberty' to entitle him to those minimum procedures appropriate under the circumstances and required by the Due Process Clause to insure that the state-created right is not arbitrarily abrogated."

Which procedures satisfy due process depends upon the nature of the government function involved and the private interest that has been affected by governmental action.

> Prison disciplinary proceedings . . . take place in a closed, tightly controlled environment peopled by those who have chosen to violate the criminal law and who have been lawfully incarcerated for doing so. . . . The reality is that disciplinary hearings and the imposition of disagreeable sanctions necessarily involve confrontations between inmates . . . who are being disciplined and those who would charge or furnish evidence against them. Retaliation is much more than a theoretical possibility; and the basic and unavoidable

task of providing reasonable personal safety for guards and inmates may be at stake, to say nothing of the impact of disciplinary confrontations and the resulting escalation of personal antagonisms on the important aims of the correctional process.

Against this background, the Court concluded that due process requires that "written notice of the charges must be given to the disciplinary action defendant in order to inform him of the charges and to enable him to marshal the facts and prepare a defense." Additionally, the disciplinary body must provide a written statement as to the evidence relied upon and reasons for the disciplinary action. "[T]he inmate facing disciplinary proceedings should [also] be allowed to call witnesses and present documentary evidence in his defense when permitting him to do so will not be unduly hazardous to institutional safety or correctional goals."

The Court concluded that due process did not require that a disciplinary defendant have an opportunity to confront and cross-examine the witnesses against him. It reasoned that the high risk of reprisal against guard or inmate accusers and the hostility in the prison that would be generated if accusers were identified justified that conclusion. The Court stated that generally speaking no right to counsel exists at disciplinary hearings. But "[w]here an illiterate inmate is involved, . . . or where the complexity of the issue makes it unlikely that the inmate will be able to collect and present the evidence necessary for an adequate comprehension of the case, he should be free to seek the aid of a fellow inmate, or if that is forbidden, to have adequate substitute aid in the form of help from the staff or from a sufficiently competent inmate designated by the staff."

Additionally, the Court held that the three-member disciplinary committee was sufficiently impartial to satisfy due process. The committee's discretion to impose discipline was limited; thus the Court concluded that the likelihood of arbitrary decision making was small.

Regarding the challenged mail regulation, the Court noted that it did not constitute a form of censorship because the mail would not be read but only opened in the presence of inmates. "The possibility that contraband will be enclosed in letters, even those from apparent attorneys, surely warrants prison officials in opening the letters." Accordingly, the Court concluded that the regulation violated no First Amendment guarantees of free speech or the Sixth Amendment right to counsel.

With regard to the regulation concerning legal assistance, the narrow issue raised was whether the state must provide or permit reasonable legal assistance to inmates for the preparation of civil rights suits. In *Johnson* v. *Avery*, 393 U.S. 483 (1969), the Court concluded that due process required that inmates be permitted to furnish each other assistance in preparing habeas corpus petitions unless the state provided reasonable alternative assistance. In this case, the challenged regulation had been interpreted to bar inmates from assisting each other in the preparation of habeas corpus and civil rights suits. Whether or not the single legal advisor made available to inmates under the regulation satisfied the requirements of *Johnson* v. *Avery* would be determined by the district court on remand. The question in this case was whether in making that determination the district court should consider the needs of inmates in filing both civil rights and habeas corpus suits.

The Court stated that "[t]he right of access to the courts, upon which *Avery* was premised, is founded in the Due Process Clause and assures that no person will be denied the opportunity to present to the judiciary allegations concerning violations of fundamental constitutional rights. It is futile to contend that the Civil Rights Act has less importance in our constitutional scheme than does the Great Writ." Accordingly, the Court concluded that the legal needs of inmates in preparing civil rights suits must be considered by the district court on remand because the rationale of *Avery* requires that inmates be permitted reasonable legal assistance in preparing such suits.

O'Brien v. *Skinner*, 414 U.S. 524 (1974)

Facts: Under a New York statute, certain incarcerated individuals who were eligible to vote were denied the right to register and vote by absentee or other procedures. In contrast, New York allows other qualified voters to register and vote by absentee procedures if they are unable to appear personally because of illness or physical disability, or because of their "duties, occupation or business." Additionally, an individual incarcerated in a county jail outside of his county of residence is permitted to vote absentee. Those incarcerated individuals denied the right to vote through absentee measures claimed that such denial arbitrarily discriminated against them in violation of equal protection.

Question: Does New York law violate equal protection by arbitrarily discriminating against incarcerated qualified voters in failing to provide them with absentee voting measures while doing so for other qualified voters?

Decision: Yes. Opinion by Chief Justice Burger. Vote: 7–2, Blackmun and Rehnquist dissenting.

Reasons: New York's election statutes discriminate among categories of qualified voters in a way that is wholly arbitrary:

> New York extends absentee *registration* privileges to eligible citizens who are unable to appear personally because of "illness or physical disability," and to citizens required to be outside their counties of residence on normal registration days because of their "duties, occupation or business." In addition, New York extends absentee *voting* privileges to those voters unable to get to the polls because of illness or physical disability, to those who are inmates of veterans' bureau hospitals, and to those who are absent from their home county on election day either because of "duties, occupation or business" or vacation. Indeed, those held in jail awaiting trial in a county other than their residence are also permitted to register by mail and vote by absentee ballot. Yet persons confined for the same reason in the county of their residence are completely denied the ballot. The New York statutes, as construed, operate as a restriction which is "so severe as to constitute an unconstitutionally onerous burden on the . . . exercise of the franchise."

Richardson v. Ramirez, 418 U.S. 24 (1974)

Facts: Three individuals who had been convicted of felonies and had completed their prison terms and paroles brought a class action claiming that provisions of California law which disfranchised persons convicted of "infamous crimes" violated the equal protection clause of the Fourteenth Amendment. The Supreme Court of California held the challenged provisions unconstitutional "as applied to all ex-felons whose terms of incarceration and parole have expired. . . ."

Question: Do state laws disenfranchising ex-felons who have completed their prison sentences and paroles violate the equal protection clause?

Decision: No. Opinion by Justice Rehnquist. Vote: 6–3, Douglas, Brennan, and Marshall dissenting.

Reasons: The equal protection clause is found in section 1 of the Fourteenth Amendment. Section 2 of that amendment authorizes Congress to reduce a state's representation in Congress for denying the franchise to male citizens twenty-one years of age or more unless that denial is based upon "participation in rebellion or other crime." Thus, section 2 expressly exempts from the sanction of reduced representation disfranchisement grounded upon prior conviction of a felony. In the absence of persuasive constitutional history to the contrary, the equal protection clause in section 1 of the Fourteenth Amendment should not be interpreted "to prohibit outright . . . that which was expressly exempted from the lesser sanction of reduced representation imposed by section 2. . . ." The history of the Fourteenth Amendment supports the conclusion that it was not intended to prohibit disfranchisement of ex-felons. Accordingly, disfranchisement of ex-felons does not violate equal protection. The general rule that denial of the franchise can only be justified under the equal protection clause by showing a "compelling state interest" does not apply in this case because the "exclusion of felons from the vote has an affirmative sanction in section 2 of the Fourteenth Amendment. . . ."

Wingo v. *Wedding*, 418 U.S. 461 (1974)

Facts: The Federal Magistrates Act authorizes federal district courts to assign to federal magistrates duties that are "not inconsistent with the Constitution and laws of the United States." Pursuant to the act, a district court adopted a local rule that provided, in part, for a magistrate in habeas corpus proceedings involving state prisoners to take evidence when he deemed it necessary to decide a habeas corpus petition and to make a recommendation for the disposition thereof to an appropriate district judge. All testimony would be electronically recorded. However, upon the request of any party, the district court would be required under the rule to hear the recording of the testimony and give it *de novo* consideration. A state prisoner challenged the validity of these provisions authorizing magistrates to conduct evidentiary hearings in habeas corpus cases on the ground, *inter alia*, that they were inconsistent with 28 U.S. Code, 2243. That section provides that an application for a writ of habeas corpus shall be entertained by a "court, justice or judge. . . ."

Question: Are the challenged provisions of the district court's local rule authorizing magistrates to hold evidentiary hearings invalid because they are inconsistent with section 2243?

Decision: Yes. Opinion by Justice Brennan. Vote: 7–2, Burger and White dissenting.

Reasons: Under the predecessor acts to section 2243, Supreme Court decisions in *Holiday* v. *Johnston*, 313 U.S. 342 (1941), and *Brown* v. *Allen*, 344 U.S. 443 (1953), clearly held that a prisoner has a right to testify before a judge in habeas corpus proceedings. "[N]othing in the text or legislative history of the Magistrates Act suggests that Congress meant to change that requirement." Accordingly, "since section 2243 requires that the District Judge personally hold evidentiary hearings in federal habeas corpus cases, [the challenged rule], insofar as it authorizes the full-time Magistrate to hold such hearings, is invalid because it is 'inconsistent with the . . . laws of the United States. . . .' "

The Court concluded that review by magistrates of applications for post-trial relief is limited to review for the purpose of proposing, not holding, evidentiary hearings. In that connection, magistrates may receive the state court records and all affidavits. stipulations and other documents submitted by the parties.

Schools and Colleges

In the field of public education, the Court's most important decisions concerned racial discrimination. The decision with the greatest public impact concerned the power of a federal district court to order cross-district busing as a remedy for desegregating the overwhelmingly black Detroit public school system. Similar plans were being considered by several other district courts and Congress was considering anti-busing legislation when a closely divided Court handed down its 5–4 decision on the last day of the term. It held that district courts lack authority to order the consolidation of school districts as part of a desegregation plan unless it can be shown that segregation in one school district was a "substantial cause" of segregation in the other districts. Although the decision seemed to defuse anti-busing sentiment, those sentiments could be reactivated if plaintiffs are able to prove the type of connection between segregation in two or more school districts that the Court held would justify cross-district busing.

In its last term the Court divided 4–4 over the issue of whether a federal district court had the power to order two adjacent white school districts to participate in a plan to desegregate the public schools of Richmond, Virginia. Justice Powell did not participate in that case, and his vote was the swing vote against general cross-district busing in the Detroit case.

In another case that sharply divided public opinion, the Court avoided a decision that could have had widespread significance for affirmative action programs designed to aid blacks and other minority groups. The case arose when DeFunis, a white applicant to the Washington state law school, was denied admission although he rated higher on the normal admissions criteria than several minority students who had been admitted. DeFunis sued claiming that the state admissions policy of preferring minority students over white students constituted racial discrimination in violation of the Fourteenth

Amendment. As the lawsuit proceeded to the Supreme Court, De-Funis was permitted to attend the Washington state law school by virtue of an order issued by Justice Douglas. When the case reached the Supreme Court, numerous amicus curiae briefs were filed on behalf of both parties. Those who defended the challenged admissions policy claimed it was necessary to overcome years of past discrimination against minorities which had handicapped them in competing on equal terms with whites. Opponents of the policy argued that discriminating against persons on the basis of race could not be justified under a Constitution which mandated equal protection of the laws. The Court never reached the merits of the case because it held that it had become moot during its three-year course of litigation. In a hotly divided 5–4 decision, the Court reasoned that since DeFunis would graduate at the end of the academic year irrespective of the outcome of his appeal, a decision on the merits would have no practical effect.

Many suspected that the Court had used the mootness issue to escape a very difficult legal and social question. That suspicion was heightened by the fact that only one week earlier, the Court had held in *Super Tire Engineering Co.* v. *McCorkle*, 416 U.S. 115 (1974), that the termination of a strike did not render a certain labor dispute moot because a decision on the merits would have continuing significance for collective bargaining. It would seem difficult to deny that a decision on the merits in the *DeFunis* case would also have had continuing significance for the admissions policies of state-operated schools.

In two other decisions, the Court expanded the rights of those attacking racial discrimination. In a unanimous decision, the Court held that federal law required the San Francisco school system to provide non-English-speaking students of Chinese ancestry instruction in a language they understand. In another unanimous opinion, the Court ruled that a federal law could be applied to permit the award of attorneys' fees to plaintiffs in desegregation cases even though the attorneys' services were rendered prior to the law's enactment.

In a case that raised issues concerning the constitutionality of federal aid to parochial schools, the Court avoided deciding any constitutional questions and ruled that certain federal funds made available under the Elementary and Secondary Education Act of 1965 must be used to provide "comparable" aid to both public and private school children. The Court's decision gave some hope to supporters of federal and state aid to parochial schools that such aid might be constitutional. Last term, in *Committee for Public Education and Religious Liberty* v. *Nyquist*, 413 U.S. 756 (1973), *Levitt* v. *Committee for*

Public Education and Religious Liberty, 413 U.S. 472 (1973), and
Sloan v. *Lemon*, 413 U.S. 825 (1973), the Court interpreted the establishment clause of the First Amendment to preclude virtually any
state aid to parochial schools.

Milliken v. *Bradley*, 418 U.S. 717 (1974)

Facts: After finding that the actions of federal, state and local
officials had caused segregation within the Detroit public school system, a federal district court concluded that a Detroit-only desegregation plan would cause "white flight" and thus would not in fact
desegregate the schools. Accordingly, the district court ordered that
a desegregation plan be designed that would include fifty-three overwhelmingly white suburban school districts containing some five hundred thousand students and that would require the purchase of 295
additional school buses. Although failing to find that the fifty-three
suburban school districts had committed acts of de jure segregation,
the district court reasoned that it nevertheless had authority to order
interdistrict relief because (1) the state of Michigan had committed
acts of de jure segregation, and (2) under Michigan law, the state has
complete authority over education including the power to control local school districts.

Question: Did the district court have constitutional authority to
issue its interdistrict desegregation order?

Decision: No. Opinion by Chief Justice Burger. Vote: 5–4, Douglas, Brennan, White, and Marshall dissenting.

Reasons: In school desegregation cases, federal remedial power
may be exercised only after a finding of a constitutional violation. The
nature of the constitutional violation determines the scope of the
remedy. In this case, the district court remedy to desegregate Detroit
schools

> would require, in effect, consolidation of 54 independent
> school-districts historically administered as separate units
> into a vast new super school district. . . . Entirely apart from
> the logistical and other serious problems attending large-
> scale transportation of students, the consolidation would
> give rise to an array of other problems in financing and op-
> erating this new school system. Some of the more obvious
> questions would be: What would be the status and authority
> of the present popularly elected school boards? Would the
> children of Detroit be within the jurisdiction and operating
> control of a school board elected by the parents and resi-

dents of other districts? What board or boards would levy taxes for school operations in these 54 districts constituting the consolidated metropolitan area? . . . What body would determine that portion of the curricula now left to the discretion of local school boards?

These problems would not in themselves have precluded the district court's interdistrict desegregation remedy. However, "[b]efore the boundaries of separate and autonomous school districts may be set aside by consolidating the separate units for remedial purposes or by imposing a cross district remedy, it must first be shown that there has been a constitutional violation within one district that produces a significant segregative effect in another district. Specifically it must be shown that racially discriminatory acts of the state or local school districts, or of a single school district, have been a substantial cause of inter-district segregation." The district court's order was improper because unsupported by the findings needed to justify an interdistrict desegregation plan.

DeFunis v. *Odegaard*, 416 U.S. 312 (1974)

Facts: Having been denied admission to the state-operated University of Washington Law School, a white applicant (DeFunis) brought suit claiming that the procedures and criteria used by the Law School Admissions Committee (which favored applicants of minority races) were racially discriminatory in violation of the equal protection clause. A state court agreed with DeFunis's claim and ordered his admission to the law school in 1971. On appeal, the Washington Supreme Court reversed, holding that the challenged law school admissions policy did not violate the Constitution. Mr. Justice Douglas stayed the judgment of the Washington Supreme Court pending final disposition by the United States Supreme Court. During oral argument before the U.S. Supreme Court on 26 February 1974, it was learned that DeFunis had registered for his final quarter in law school and that he would be awarded his law degree at the end of the academic year irrespective of the outcome of his appeal. The Court on its own motion raised the question whether the case had thus become moot.

Question: Is the case moot and thus beyond federal jurisdiction?

Decision: Yes. Per curiam opinion. Vote: 5–4, Douglas, Brennan, White, and Marshall dissenting.

Reasons: Article III of the Constitution limits the jurisdiction of the federal courts to concrete cases and controversies. Federal courts have no jurisdiction to review moot cases. A case in federal court is moot if a decision would not affect the rights of the litigants. This case is moot because "all parties agree that DeFunis is now entitled to complete his legal studies at the University of Washington and to receive his degree from that institution. A determination by this Court of the legal issues tendered by the parties is no longer necessary to compel that result, and could not serve to prevent it." Reasoning that similar cases could proceed with relative speed, the Court concluded that this case did not fall within the doctrine permitting federal adjudication of an otherwise moot case if it presented a question that would probably be repeated but was likely to evade judicial review.

Lau v. Nichols, 414 U.S. 563 (1974)

Facts: The San Francisco public school system failed to provide English language instruction to approximately eighteen hundred students of Chinese ancestry who did not speak English. Those eighteen hundred students brought suit in federal district court claiming that the failure to provide them with English language instruction violated section 601 of the Civil Rights Act of 1964. That section bans discrimination based "on the ground of race, color, or national origin," in "any program or activity receiving federal financial assistance." It was established in the district court that the San Francisco school system received large amounts of federal financial assistance and thus fell within the coverage of section 601.

Question: Does section 601 of the Civil Rights Act of 1964 require the San Francisco school system to provide non-English-speaking students of Chinese ancestry with instruction in a language they understand?

Decision: Yes. Opinion by Justice Douglas. Vote: 9--0.

Reasons: Under section 602 of the act, the Department of Health, Education and Welfare (HEW) has authority to issue rules and regulations to assure that recipients of federal aid comply with the anti-discrimination provisions of section 601. HEW has interpreted one of its validly issued regulations to require that school districts take "affirmative steps" to rectify the language deficiency of non-English-speaking "national origin-minority group children." Obviously, the Chinese-speaking minority benefits less than the English-speaking majority from the San Francisco school system. In fact, the failure to instruct the Chinese-speaking children in a language they understand "denies them a meaningful opportunity to participate in the education program—all earmarks of the discrimination banned by the

[HEW] regulations." The Court noted that the illegal discrimination might be remedied either by instructing the students of Chinese ancestry in Chinese or by teaching them English.

Bradley v. School Board of Richmond, 416 U.S. 696 (1974)

Facts: Successful plaintiffs in a protracted desegregation suit against the school board of Richmond, Virginia, were awarded attorneys' fees for services rendered from 10 March 1970 to 29 January 1971. During appellate review of the award, Congress enacted section 718 of the Education Amendments Act of 1972 which grants a federal court discretionary authority to award attorneys' fees to a successful desegregation plaintiff upon a finding that the suit "was necessary to bring about compliance" with the Constitution or the Civil Rights Act of 1964. The court of appeals held that the award of attorneys' fees was erroneous, concluding, *inter alia*, that section 718 did not apply to the services rendered in this case.

Question: Does section 718 apply to attorneys' services rendered before its enactment in a situation where the propriety of the fee award is pending appellate resolution at the time of its enactment?

Decision: Yes. Opinion by Justice Blackmun. Vote: 7–0. Marshall and Powell did not participate.

Reasons: The Court stated, "We anchor our holding in this case on the principle that a court is to apply the law in effect at the time it renders its decision, unless doing so would result in manifest injustice or there is statutory direction or legislative history to the contrary." The legislative history of section 718 seems "to provide at least implicit support for the application of the statute to pending cases." Accordingly, section 718 should be applied to pending cases unless it would cause manifest injustice. The existence of manifest injustice must be determined by considering the nature and identity of the parties, the nature of their rights, and the impact upon those rights by a change in law.

In this case, the defendant school board had greater resources than the plaintiffs and had the constitutional duty to desegregate. The school board had no matured right to nonpayment of attorneys' fees when section 718 was enacted. Finally, the application of section 718 to sustain the award of attorneys' fees would not change the substantive obligation of the school board to desegregate but "merely serves to create an additional basis or source for the Board's potential obligation to pay attorneys' fees. . . . Accordingly, upon considering the parties, the nature of the rights, and the impact of section 718 upon those rights, it cannot be said that the application of the statute to an award of fees for services rendered prior to its effective date, in an action pending on that date, would cause 'manifest injustice. . . .' "

The Court also concluded that section 718 permitted recovery of attorneys' fees at least up to the date of a final court order which in this case was 5 April 1971. The case was thus remanded to permit the district court in its discretion to award reasonable attorneys' fees for services rendered from 10 March 1970 to or beyond 5 April 1971.

Gilmore v. City of Montgomery, Ala., 417 U.S. 556 (1974)

Facts: In 1958, a federal district court ordered the city of Montgomery, Alabama, to desegregate its public parks, and it retained jurisdiction over the case. In 1971, Negro citizens moved for a supplemental order alleging that the city was permitting racially segregated schools and other segregated private groups and clubs to use city parks and recreational facilities. After making certain findings, the district court enjoined the city from permitting the use of its recreational facilities by any private school group or other private groups practicing racial discrimination. With regard to the prohibition against the use of city facilities by racially segregated private schools, the district court reasoned that such use would enhance the attractiveness of those schools and thus be inconsistent with the city's duty to maintain a desegregated school system. On appeal, the court of appeals reversed in part the district court order, and substantially narrowed the scope of the injunction. It sustained that part of the injunction which restrained the use of city facilities by segregated private schools when that use was "exclusive" and not in common with other citizens. The court of appeals ruled, however, that "nonexclusive enjoyment" of those facilities by private school children in segregated schools was not a sufficient threat to the maintenance of a desegregated public school system to support an injunction restraining their use of such facilities. The court of appeals also concluded that the injunction against use of city recreational facilities by racially segregated, private nonschool groups was improper, because it was not proven that the city was substantially involved in the support of the racially discriminatory policies of those groups.

Question: Was it proper for the court of appeals to reverse in part the district court order?

Decision: Yes. Opinion by Justice Blackmun. Vote: 8–1, Marshall dissenting in part.

Reasons: The equal protection clause of the Fourteenth Amendment bars the government from directly or indirectly supporting or encouraging racial discrimination. However, that clause does not bar racial discrimination practiced solely by private individuals or groups.

In this case, the court of appeals properly affirmed the district court order insofar as it enjoined the "exclusive" use of the city's recreational facilities by racially segregated private schools. The city had an affirmative duty to eliminate every vestige of its formerly segregated facilities by virtue of the 1958 district court order. By granting exclusive use of its formerly segregated recreational facilities to racially segregated private schools, the city would be violating that duty. Moreover, granting such exclusive use would directly contravene an outstanding school desegregation order by encouraging the perpetuation of a dual school system. "[A]ny tangible state assistance, outside the generalized services government might provide to private segregated schools in common with other schools, and with all citizens, is constitutionally prohibited if it has 'a significant tendency to facilitate, reinforce, and support private discrimination.' "

With regard to whether nonexclusive use of the city's recreational facilities by racially segregated private schools should be enjoined, the record developed by the district court is insufficient to justify a final conclusion at this stage. Such relief will be appropriate if the district court makes findings upon remand such that either the use directly impairs the outstanding school desegregation order or constitutes a vestige of the type of state-sponsored segregation of the city's recreational facilities that was condemned in the 1958 decree.

"The problem of [racially segregated] private [nonschool] group use is much more complex." An injunction against such use would be proper if "there is significant state involvement in the private discrimination alleged. . . . Traditional state monopolies, such as electricity, water, and police and fire protection—all generalized governmental services—do not by their mere provision constitute a showing of state involvement in invidious discrimination. . . . The same is true of a broad spectrum of municipal recreational facilities: parks, playgrounds, athletic facilities, amphitheaters, museums, zoos, and the like. . . . It follows, therefore, that the portion of the District Court's order prohibiting the mere use of such facilities by *any* segregated 'private group, club or organization' is invalid because it was not predicated upon a proper finding of state action." On remand, if the district court finds that the city has become "significantly involved" in private discrimination by making its recreational facilities available to private groups practicing racial discrimination, then enjoining such use would be proper.

Mayor of Philadelphia v. *Educational Equality League*, 415 U.S. 605 (1974)

Facts: Under the city charter, the mayor of Philadelphia is empowered to appoint a thirteen-member Educational Nominating Panel. Four members of the panel must be chosen from the citizenry at large, and the remaining nine from the highest-ranking officers of various citywide organizations. The function of the panel is to submit a number of nominees for the school board to the mayor, who must make appointments to the board from the nominees submitted. Suit was brought against Mayor Tate alleging that he had discriminated against Negroes in his appointments to the 1971 panel in violation of the equal protection clause. The district court dismissed the suit for failure to prove racial discrimination. It concluded that the small number of positions on the panel minimized the significance of the facts that Negroes constituted 34 percent of the city's population, 60 percent of the public school pupils, but only 15 percent of the 1971 panel. The court of appeals reversed, concluding that the record established a prima facie case of racial discrimination in the appointments to the 1971 panel. Although Mayor Rizzo had replaced Tate while the case was *sub judice*, the court of appeals nevertheless ordered the district court to exercise supervision over the new mayor's 1973 panel appointments to guard against racial discrimination.

Questions: Did the court of appeals err in overturning the district court's findings and conclusions of nondiscrimination? Did the court of appeals err in ordering prospective injunctive relief against the new mayor?

Decision: Yes to both questions. Opinion by Justice Powell. Vote: 5–4, Douglas, Brennan, White, and Marshall dissenting.

Reasons: The court of appeals found racial discrimination on the basis of "ambiguous testimony as to an alleged statement in 1969 by then Mayor Tate with regard to the 1969 school board, not the 1971 panel; the unawareness of certain organizations on the part of a city official who did not have final authority over or responsibility for the challenged appointments; and racial-composition percentage comparisons that we think were correctly rejected by the District Court as meaningless." Such fragmentary and speculative evidence was insufficient to prove racial discrimination.

The court of appeals also erred in ordering injunctive relief against Mayor Rizzo. Nothing in the record relates to his appointment policies regarding the Educational Nominating Panel. "Where there have been prior patterns of discrimination by the occupant of a state executive office but an intervening change in administration, the issuance of prospective coercive relief against the successor to the office must rest, at a minimum, on supplemental findings of fact indicating that the new officer will continue the practices of his predecessor."

The Court also rejected the contention made by the dissent that certain state law issues should have been decided before reaching the constitutional question. The Court concluded that the state law issues were peripheral to the main equal protection claim, were not vigorously asserted before the district court, and thus did not justify abstaining from deciding the equal protection claim.

Wheeler v. Barrera, 417 U.S. 402 (1974)

Facts: Title I of the Elementary and Secondary Education Act of 1965 provides for federal funding of special programs for educationally deprived children in both public and private schools. The special programs are administered by local public educational officials. In order to receive federal funds, the local officials must submit to a state educational agency a proposed program designed to meet the special educational needs of educationally deprived children in school attendance areas with high concentrations of children from low-income families. The state agency then must approve the local plan and, in turn, forward the approved proposal to the United States Commissioner of Education, who has the ultimate responsibility for administering the program and dispensing the appropriated and allocated funds. In order to receive state approval, the proposed plan must, *inter alia*, provide private school students with services that are "comparable in quality, scope, and opportunity for participation to those provided for public school children with needs of equally high priority."

Parents of school children attending nonpublic schools in Kansas City, Missouri, brought suit against various Missouri state education officials alleging that they were illegally and arbitrarily approving Title I funds for special programs that deprived eligible nonpublic school children of services "comparable" to those offered eligible public school children. The district court found that while most of Missouri's Title I funds were used to employ teachers to instruct in remedial subjects, the defendant state officials refused to approve any program that allocated funds to employ teachers in parochial schools. The consequence of this refusal was that substantially less money per pupil was expended for eligible students in private schools than public schools and that private school children did not receive services comparable to those received by public school children. The defendants claimed that Title I did not require that they supply on-the-premises instruction in parochial schools, and that to do so would violate Missouri law and the establishment clause of the First Amendment.

The district court denied relief. The court of appeals reversed. It concluded that (1) the defendants were operating in violation of the comparability requirement of Title I, and (2) Missouri law did not prohibit the use of public school teachers in private schools. The court abstained from deciding the question of whether the establishment clause of the First Amendment would be violated if Title I permitted use of public school teachers on private school premises because no specific plan for compliance with the comparability requirement of Title I was before it.

Question: Were the defendant state educational officials administering Title I in violation of the comparability requirement?

Decision: Yes. Opinion by Justice Blackmun. Vote: 8–1, Douglas dissenting.

Reasons: The record in this case clearly shows that the state educational officials "failed to meet their statutory commitment to provide comparable services to children in nonpublic schools." The case was remanded to the district court where the state and local officials would have an opportunity to submit a Title I plan which satisfied the comparability requirement. The Court noted that the comparability requirement of Title I might be satisfied in many ways other than the use of plans that employ teachers on private school premises. Devising such alternative plans would be the responsibility of local and state educational authorities.

The Court also concluded that the court of appeals erred in reaching the question of whether Missouri law forbade certain uses of Title I funds. It reasoned that the comparability requirement of Title I must be satisfied notwithstanding any inconsistent state law.

Finally, the Court refused to resolve any establishment clause questions that might be raised by the use of Title I funds to aid parochial schools because no particular aid program was before it.

Civil Rights and Civil Liberties

The Court decided a variety of significant cases relating to civil rights and civil liberties. The issues raised concerned defamation laws, obscenity, due process, bank records, political advertising, zoning, and the liability of certain state officials growing out of the 1970 deaths at Kent State University. The decisions revealed no pro– or anti–civil liberties tendencies on the part of the Court. Civil rights were extended in some areas and narrowed in others.

Two cases closely followed by the press concerned a so-called right-of-reply statute and the right of a private individual to sue the media for defamation. In a unanimous opinion, the Court held unconstitutional a Florida statute which afforded a candidate attacked by a newspaper a right to reply free of charge. The Court concluded that the First Amendment prohibits any governmental control over the content of a newspaper. In a related decision, the Court relaxed the barriers that previously existed to a defamation suit against the media brought by private individuals. In 1971, a plurality of the Court concluded that individuals involved in matters of "public or general concern" could recover in a defamation action against the media only upon proof that the alleged defamatory statements were made with "actual malice." This term, a divided 5–4 Court held that states could afford private individuals a remedy if the defamatory statements were negligently made. Notably, however, the Court added that such negligence could afford a recovery only of actual damages proven by findings in the record. (Many states have defamatory laws which presume that actual damages are caused by defamatory statements.) Because it may be difficult to prove that defamatory statements have caused actual injury within the community or elsewhere, the Court's decision may afford private individuals a somewhat illusory remedy.

During the 1972–73 term, in *Miller* v. *California*, 413 U.S. 15 (1973), the Court ushered in an era of tighter controls on obscenity by broadening what can be prohibited under the Constitution. In a 5–4 decision, the Court ruled that obscenity includes materials which appeal to a prurient interest in sex, which portray specifically defined sexual conduct in a patently offensive way and which, taken as a whole, lack serious literary, artistic, political, or scientific value. *Miller* also held that local standards may determine what is "prurient" or "patently offensive." The dissenters in *Miller* predicted that the new constitutional definition of obscenity would thrust the Court into the position of reviewing numerous decisions on a case-by-case basis to determine whether the particular material involved was obscene. The validity of that prediction gained some support this term when the Court unanimously ruled that the film *Carnal Knowledge* was not obscene. Because local attitudes toward the portrayal of sex vary widely thoughout the country, it seems that the Court may be forced to review many obscenity cases.

The Court this term narrowly construed previous decisions that had extended the boundaries of due process. In virtually overruling *Fuentes* v. *Shevin*, 407 U.S. 67 (1972), the Court held that a creditor could obtain a writ for the seizure of the debtor's property without giving prior notice to the debtor or providing an opportunity to be heard. *Fuentes* had concluded that due process generally requires that the debtor be given notice and a hearing before seizure of his property. In a related case, a plurality of the Court ruled that federal civil service employees could be discharged without a prior evidentiary hearing essentially on the ground that the civil service statutes informed such employees not to expect such a hearing. The rationale of the plurality opinion would virtually emasculate due process rights as enunciated in *Board of Regents* v. *Roth*, 408 U.S. 564 (1972). The rationale would seem to permit states to authorize a deprivation of property or liberty without a hearing if the possessor of the property or liberty was informed not to expect a hearing.

In an important case for law enforcement, the Court upheld the constitutionality of the recordkeeping requirements of the Bank Secrecy Act of 1970. Under that act, banks are required to maintain records of certain currency transactions and of depositors when such records will help to combat crime. Many other important constitutional issues arising under the act were left undecided because they were not considered ready for review.

Justice Douglas is generally a vigorous defender of rights asserted under the First Amendment. In two notable cases this term, however, he seemed to depart from his stated absolutist view of that amendment. In an opinion written by Douglas, the Court rejected the claim of students that a zoning ordinance forbidding the use of certain real property as a residence by more than two unrelated persons violated First Amendment rights of free association. Douglas was also the swing vote in a 5–4 decision that rejected the contention that the First Amendment forbids a city rapid transit system from refusing to accept political advertising on its vehicles.

In a decision that strengthened the effectiveness of a commonly used federal civil rights statute, 42 U.S. Code, 1983, the Court unanimously ruled that the statute afforded the higest state executive officers no absolute immunity from suit.

Miami Herald Publishing Co. v. Tornillo, 418 U.S. 241 (1974)

Facts: Florida's so-called "right of reply" statute provides a candidate for nomination or election, if assailed regarding his personal character or official record by any newspaper, the right to demand that the newspaper print, free of cost to the candidate, any reply the candidate may make to the newspaper's charges. Failure to comply with the statute constitutes a misdemeanor, and subjects the newspaper to civil damages and injunctive relief compelling the newspaper to print a candidate's reply. The Miami Herald newspaper sharply criticized a candidate for the Florida House of Representatives in editorials but refused to print his replies. In a suit brought by the candidate pursuant to Florida's right of reply statute, the Miami Herald claimed that the statute violated the freedom of the press as guaranteed by the First Amendment.

Question: Does Florida's right of reply statute violate the First Amendment?

Decision: Yes. Opinion by Chief Justice Burger. Vote: 9–0.

Reasons: Past decisions of the Supreme Court clearly imply that newspapers may not constitutionally be compelled

> to publish that which "reason" tells them should not be published. . . . Even if a newspaper would face no additional costs to comply with a compulsory access law and would not be forced to forego publication of news or opinion by the inclusion of the reply, the Florida statute fails to clear the barriers of the First Amendment because of its intrusion into the function of editors. A newspaper is more than a passive receptacle or conduit for news, comment, and advertising. The choice of material to go into a newspaper, and the decisions made as to limitations on the size of the paper, and content, and treatment of public issues and public officials—whether fair or unfair—constitutes the exercise of editorial control and judgment. It has yet to be demonstrated how governmental regulation of this crucial process can be exercised consistent with the First Amendment guarantees of a free press as they have evolved to this time.

The Court rejected the argument that increasing concentration of control of the communications media justified right of reply statutes in order to expand the "marketplace of ideas," which the First Amendment was designed to promote.

Gertz v. Welch, Inc., 418 U.S. 323 (1974)

Facts: An attorney involved in controversial litigation brought a libel suit in federal district court against a John Birch Society publication for having falsely accused him of having a criminal record and certain Communist connections. The district court dismissed the suit on the ground that the attorney failed to prove that the challenged statements were made with knowledge of their falsity or with reckless disregard for whether they were true or not (actual malice). In *New York Times* v. *Sullivan*, 376 U.S. 254 (1964), the Court held that under the First Amendment a "public official" could not constitutionally recover damages against the media in a defamation action stemming from statements concerning his official conduct unless the defamatory falsehoods were made with actual malice. In *Curtis Publishing Co.* v. *Butts*, 388 U.S. 130 (1967), and *Rosenbloom* v. *Metromedia*, 403 U.S. 29 (1971), the Court extended the *New York Times* actual malice rule to defamation actions brought by "public figures" and individuals involved in matters of "public or general concern." The district court reasoned that because the defamatory statements concerned a public issue, the actual malice rule of *New York Times* governed the defamation suit.

Question: Does the *New York Times* actual malice rule apply to defamation suits brought by an individual who is neither a public official nor a public figure?

Decision: No. Opinion by Justice Powell. Vote: 5–4, Burger, Douglas, Brennan, and White dissenting.

Reasons: "[T]here is no constitutional value in false statements of fact. . . . [But] punishment of error runs the risk of inducing a cautious and restrictive exercise of the constitutionally guaranteed freedoms of speech and press. . . . The First Amendment requires that we protect some falsehood in order to protect speech that matters."

On the other hand, the state has a legitimate interest in compensating individuals who have been injured by defamatory falsehoods. When a public person is involved, the *New York Times* actual malice rule brings about the proper constitutional accommodation between the interests of a free press and the interest in compensation for wrongful hurt to one's reputation. However, "the state interest in compensating injury to the reputation of private individuals requires that a different rule should obtain with respect to them."

Private individuals have less readily available access to the media to rebut unfair charges than do public persons. Additionally, private persons, unlike most public figures, have not voluntarily subjected their lives to the scrutiny of the media. "Thus, private individuals are not only more vulnerable to injury than public officials and public figures; they are also more deserving of recovery." Accordingly, "so long as they do not impose liability without fault, the States may define for themselves the appropriate standard of liability for a publisher or broadcaster of defamatory falsehood injurious to a private individual. . . . At least this conclusion obtains where, as here, the substance of the defamatory statement 'makes substantial danger to reputation apparent.' "

However, the state interest in permitting private individuals to recover for injury to reputation extends no further than "compensation for actual injury." States may not permit recovery by a private individual of presumed or punitive damages without proof of actual malice. "[A]ctual injury is not limited to out-of-pocket loss [and may] . . . include impairment of reputation and standing in the community, personal humiliation, and mental anguish and suffering."

In this case, the attorney plaintiff was not a "public figure" for purposes of the *New York Times* rule. Although the attorney was active in community affairs, he had achieved no general fame or notoriety. He did not "thrust himself into the vortex" of the public issue that generated the defamatory falsehoods. Accordingly, the district court erred in concluding that the *New York Times* rule applied to this case and in thus entering judgment in favor of the publisher.

Jenkins v. Georgia, 418 U.S. 153 (1974)

Facts: For showing the film *Carnal Knowledge*, a theater manager was convicted in Georgia State Court of the crime of distributing obscene material. In determining whether the film was obscene, the jurors were instructed by the trial court to apply "community standards" without specifying whether the community was national, state, or local. The manager appealed his conviction claiming that under the constitutional definition of obscenity established in *Miller* v. *California*, 413 U.S. 15 (1973), the film could not constitutionally be declared obscene.

Question: Is the film *Carnal Knowledge* protected from suppression under the First Amendment because not constitutionally obscene?

Decision: Yes. Opinion by Justice Rehnquist. Vote: 9–0.

Reasons: The Court first emphasized that under the *Miller* decision, states may constitutionally define obscenity in terms of local, state, or national community standards. It added that a state may also define obscenity in terms of "contemporary community standards" without further specification as was done in this case.

With regard to the merits, *Miller* held that one of the three constitutionally required characteristics of obscene material is that it "depicts or describes, in a patently offensive way, sexual conduct specifically defined by the applicable state law." Having viewed the film, the Court found that it was not "patently offensive." The Court noted that

> [w]hile the subject matter of the picture is, in a broader sense, sex, and there are scenes in which sexual conduct including "ultimate sexual acts" is to be understood to be taking place, the camera does not focus on the bodies of the actors at such times. . . . There are occasional scenes of nudity, but nudity alone is not enough to make material legally obscene under the *Miller* standards.

In a related case concerning a federal statute prohibiting the mailing of obscene material, *Hamling* v. *United States*, 418 U.S. 87 (1974), the Court held that obscenity under federal statutes could be determined on the basis of local community standards. This decision may subject distributors of allegedly obscene material to varying community standards in the various federal judicial districts into which they transmit material.

Mitchell v. *W. T. Grant Co.*, 416 U.S. 600 (1974)

Facts: Louisiana statutes permit a plaintiff-creditor claiming a security interest in certain property to secure a writ ordering sequestration of that property before final judgment "if it is within the power of the defendant to conceal, dispose of, or waste the property . . . or remove the property from the parish [in which the suit is brought], during the pendency of the action." The writ of sequestration may be issued "only when the nature of the claim and the amount thereof, if any, and the grounds relied upon for the issuance of the writ clearly appear from specific facts" as shown by a verified petition or affidavit. With respect to the parish involved in this case, only a judge can authorize a writ of sequestration and only after a creditor files a sufficient bond to protect the defendant against certain damages. Although the writ is obtainable on the creditor's ex parte application, without notice to debtor or opportunity for a hearing, the debtor may obtain immediate dissolution of the writ unless the creditor "proves the grounds upon which the writ issued." The defendant-debtor may also regain possession of the sequestered property by filing a bond to protect the creditor against damage if the creditor ultimately wins the lawsuit.

A creditor filed suit against a debtor in the New Orleans City Court to recover the overdue balance of the price of certain personal property which the creditor had sold to the debtor and in which it held a security interest. As authorized by Louisiana statutes, the creditor obtained a writ ordering sequestration of the personal property without notice to the debtor or opportunity for a hearing. The debtor unsuccessfully sought repossession of the sequestered property on the ground that the Louisiana sequestration procedures violated the due process clause of the Fourteenth Amendment.

Question: On the facts of this case did the Louisana sequestration procedure violate due process?

Decision: No. Opinion by Justice White. Vote: 5–4, Stewart, Douglas, Marshall, and Brennan dissenting.

Reasons: The debtor contends that "because he had possession of and a substantial interest in the sequestered property, the Due Process Clause of the Fourteenth Amendment necessarily forbade the seizure without prior notice and opportunity for a hearing." In this case, however, both the "seller and buyer had current real interests in the property, and the definition of property rights is a matter of state law. Resolution of the due process question must take account not only of the interests of the buyer of the property but those of the seller as well." The seller had an interest in preventing deterioration in the ratio of value of the secured property to the unpaid debt.

> Wholly aside from whether the buyer, with possession and power over the property, will destroy or make away with the goods, the buyer in possession of consumer goods will undeniably put the property to its intended use, and the resale value of the merchandise will steadily decline as it is used over a period of time. Any installment seller anticipates as much, but he is normally protected because the buyer's installment payments keep pace with the deterioration in value of the security. Clearly, if payments cease and possession and use by the buyer continue, the seller's interest in the property as security is steadily and irretrievably eroded until the time at which the full hearing is held.

Additionally, notice to the buyer before issuance of a sequestration writ would permit him to conceal or transfer the merchandise to the detriment of the seller.

The buyer has an interest in maintaining possession of the purchased property before notice is given and there is an opportunity for a hearing. However, that interest is outweighed by "his inability to make the creditor whole for wrongful possession, the risk of destruction or alienation if notice and a prior hearing are supplied, and the low risk of a wrongful determination of possession through the procedures now employed." In addition, "the debtor may immediately have a full hearing on the matter of possession following the execution of the writ, thus cutting to a bare minimum the time of creditor or court supervised possession. . . . Considering the Louisiana procedure as a whole, we are convinced that the State has reached a constitutional accommodation of the respective interests of buyer and seller."

The Court distinguished its recent decision in *Fuentes* v. *Shevin*, 407 U.S. 67 (1972), which held that Florida and Pennsylvania replevin statutes permitting a secured installment seller to repossess goods sold without notice or hearing were unconstitutional. The Court stated that the following differences between the statutes challenged in *Fuentes* and the challenged Louisiana statutes were relevant to the due process question:

> The *Fuentes* statutes (1) permitted an order of repossession to be issued by a court clerk rather than a judge; (2) failed to permit the buyer an immediate hearing on whether the order was validly issued; (3) failed to require the seller to state his claim in detail by affidavit; and (4) possessed a higher risk that property would be improperly repossessed because proof of "wrongful" detention was necessary to secure the repossession order.

Arnett v. *Kennedy*, 416 U.S. 134 (1974)

Facts: A federal employee in the competitive civil service was discharged under 5 U.S. Code, 7501(a) for charging two of his superiors with misconduct, including bribery, allegedly with no basis in fact. Section 7501(a) provides that "[a]n individual in the competitive service may be removed . . . only for such cause as will promote the efficiency of the service." The employee was entitled to notice of the charges lodged against him and an opportunity to respond orally and in writing before discharge under section 7501(b). Additionally, the employee had a right to appeal the validity of his discharge to the Civil Service Commission where he would be entitled to an evidentiary, trial type of hearing. An employee who is reinstated after a wrongful discharge receives full back pay. Declining to take advantage of the administrative procedures available to him, the discharged employee sued in federal district court claiming that he was unconstitutionally discharged. He contended that (1) the discharge procedures violated due process in failing to provide for a trial-type hearing before an impartial agency prior to removal, and (2) section 7501 was unconstitutionally vague in failing to furnish sufficiently precise guidelines as to what kind of speech may justify removal.

Questions: (1) Do the administrative procedures afforded federal employees discharged under section 7501(a) violate due process? (2) Is section 7501(a) unconstitutionally vague?

Decision: No to both questions. Opinion by Justice Rehnquist. Vote: 5–4 on the first question and 6–3 on the second. White dissented as to the first question; Douglas, Marshall, and Brennan dissented on both.

Reasons: Board of Regents v. *Roth,* 408 U.S. 564 (1972), established the proposition that a property interest protected by due process must be defined in terms of rules or understandings that stem from a nonconstitutional source such as state or federal law. In this case, the federal employee

> did have a statutory expectancy that he not be removed other than for "such cause as will promote the efficiency of the service." But the very section of the statute which granted him that right, a right which had previously existed only by virtue of administrative regulation, expressly provided also for the procedure by which "cause" was to be determined, and expressly omitted the procedural guarantees which [the employee] insists are mandated by the Constitution. Only by bifurcating the very sentence of the Act of Congress which conferred upon [the employee] the right not to be removed save for cause could it be said that he had an expectancy of that substantive right without the procedural limitations which Congress attached to it.

Section 7501 may not be so parsed. Accordingly, under section 7501 an employee acquires an interest in employment limited by the procedures that Congress has designated for removal. Under *Roth,* that interest was not entitled to constitutional protection under the due process clause.

The Court also rejected the claim that discharging an employee upon an accusation of dishonesty without a prior hearing would cause such a loss of reputation as to constitute a deprivation of "liberty" without due process. The Court reasoned that the employee could vindicate his reputation on appeal before the Civil Service Commission and that the delays in processing an appeal were not sufficiently long to cause impingement of any liberty interest.

Regarding the claim that section 7501(a) is unconstitutionally vague, the Court noted that it must be considered in light of the practice of the employee's agency to provide advice on the interpretation of section 7501(a) and implementing regulations.

The phrase "such cause as will promote the efficiency of

the service" as a standard of employee job protection is without doubt intended to authorize dismissal for speech as well as other conduct. . . . Because of the infinite variety of factual situations in which public statements by government employees might reasonably justify dismissal for "cause," . . . [section 7501(a)] describes, as explicitly as is required, the employee conduct which is grounds for removal.

In response to the contention that section 7501(a) would operate to chill or punish the exercise of constitutionally protected speech, the Court stated that it "proscribes only that public speech which improperly damages and impairs the reputation and efficiency of the employing agency, and it thus imposes no greater controls on the behavior of federal employees than are necessary for the protection of the Government as an employer."

California Bankers Association v. *Shultz,* 416 U.S. 21 (1974)

Facts: Various plaintiffs brought suit challenging the constitutionality of the Bank Secrecy Act of 1970 and certain implementing regulations. The plaintiffs included a banker's association, an individual bank, bank depositors, and the American Civil Liberties Union (ACLU). They attacked Title I and Title II of the act and their implementing regulations on the grounds that they violated (1) the Fourth Amendment protection against unreasonable searches and seizures, (2) the Fifth Amendment privilege against self-incrimination, and (3) the First Amendment right of free speech and association.

Title I of the act generally requires banks to record the identities of persons having accounts with them and of persons having signature authority. Upon the secretary of the treasury's determination by regulation that such records would have a "high degree of usefulness" for law enforcement purposes, the banks must make and maintain microfilm or other reproductions of each check, draft, or other instrument drawn on it and presented to it for payment, and must maintain a record of each check, draft, or other instrument received by it for deposit or collection, together with an identification of the party for whose account it is to be deposited or collected. Title I further authorizes the secretary to require banks to maintain a record of the identity of all individuals who engage in transactions which are reportable by the bank under Title II of the act, and to prescribe the required retention period for such records.

By regulation, the secretary exempted checks of $100 or less from the copying requirements of Title I. Other regulations require banks to maintain (1) records of the identity and taxpayer identification number of each person maintaining a financial interest in each deposit or share account opened after 30 June 1972 and to microfilm various other financial documents; (2) a microfilm or other copy of each extension of credit in an amount exceeding $5 thousand except those secured by interest in real property; and (3) a microfilm of each advice, request, or instruction given or received regarding the transfer of funds, currency, or other money or credit in amounts exceeding $10 thousand to a person, account or place outside the United States. The regulations also provide that inspection of or access to these records is governed by existing legal process.

Title II of the act and the regulations promulgated thereunder generally require (1) persons to report transportations of monetary instruments into or out of the United States, or receipts of such instruments in the United States from places outside the United States, if the transportation or receipt involves instruments of a value greater than $5 thousand, and (2) United States citizens, residents, and businessmen to file reports of their relationships with foreign financial institutions.

Question: Are any of the provisions of the Bank Secrecy Act or implementing regulations as applied to these plaintiffs unconstitutional?

Decision: No. Opinion by Justice Rehnquist. Vote: 6–3, Douglas, Brennan, and Marshall dissenting.

Reasons: "[T]he bank plaintiffs [contend] that the recordkeeping requirements imposed by the Secretary's regulations under the authority of Title I deprive the banks of due process by imposing unreasonable burdens upon them, and by seeking to make the banks the agents of the Government in surveillance of its citizens." Similar recordkeeping requirements imposed upon countless businesses subject to the Price Control Act during World War II and upon employers subject to the Fair Labor Standards Act have been upheld because they were rationally related to federal enforcement objectives. In this case, the bank records required under the Bank Secrecy Act are rationally related to aiding the enforcement of federal tax, regulatory, and criminal laws and thus satisfy due process requirements.

Banks and depositors contend that the recordkeeping requirements under Title I of the act violate the Fourth Amendment rights on the theory that the secretary "seizes" records of bank customers by requiring that they be maintained. That claim must be rejected, because it is well established that a summons issued against a third party does not violate the Fourth Amendment rights of a person under investigation. Because no such attempt had been made, the Court declined to decide whether the secretary could lawfully gain access to bank records maintained under Title I without a warrant or notice to the person under investigation.

The claim that the Title I recordkeeping requirements violated the Fifth Amendment privilege was rejected. The Court concluded that the privilege was not available to incorporated banks or other organizations. Regarding bank depositors, the Court ruled that "a party incriminated by evidence produced by a third party sustains no violation of his own Fifth Amendment rights."

The Court also rejected the claim that the foreign reporting requirements under Title II of the act violated the Fourth Amendment. Comparing the reporting requirements to those requiring persons to file income tax returns, the Court concluded that "[i]f reporting of income may be required as an aid to enforcement of the federal revenue statutes, and if those entering and leaving the country may be examined as to their belongings and effects, all without violating the Fourth Amendment, we see no reason to invalidate the Secretary's regulations here."

The claim that the domestic reporting requirements under Title II of the act violated the Fourth Amendment, the Court stated, must be considered in light of the reporting that the secretary has in fact required and not what the act might authorize him to require. Such requirements are reasonable:

> The regulations require the reporting of information with respect to abnormally large transactions in currency, much of which information the bank as a party to the transaction already possesses or would acquire in its own interest. To the extent that the regulations in connection with such transactions require the bank to obtain information from a customer simply because the Government wants it, the information is sufficiently described and limited in nature, and sufficiently related to a tenable congressional determination as to improper use of transactions of that type in interstate commerce, so as to withstand the Fourth Amendment challenge made by the bank plaintiffs.

The Court refused to consider the Fourth Amendment claim concerning the domestic reporting regulations asserted by plaintiff depositors because none had alleged that reports of his transactions were required.

The Court also declined to rule on the following claims attacking various provisions of the act, because the record did not disclose that those provisions had caused the plaintiffs injury or threatened them with immediate injury: (1) whether the foreign and domestic reporting requirements violate a bank depositor's Fifth Amendment privilege against self-incrimination, (2) whether a depositor must be notified if a summons is issued to their bank demanding access to records containing information concerning the depositor, and (3) whether compelled disclosure of the bank records required to be maintained under the act would violate the depositor's First Amendment right of associational freedom by breaching the confidentiality of many associations.

Village of Belle Terre v. *Boraas*, 416 U.S. 1 (1974)

Facts: A New York village ordinance restricts certain land use to one-family dwellings while excluding lodging houses, boarding houses, fraternity houses, or multiple dwelling houses. The word "family" for purposes of the ordinance is defined as one or more persons related by blood, adoption, or marriage, or not more than two unrelated persons, living and cooking together as a single housekeeping unit. The owners of a house in the village and three of the six student tenants of the house challenged the constitutionality of the village zoning ordinance on the grounds that it violated equal protection and constitutional rights of association, travel, and privacy.

Question: Is the challenged zoning ordinance unconstitutional?

Decision: No. Opinion by Justice Douglas. Vote: 7–2, Brennan and Marshall dissenting.

Reasons: In *Euclid* v. *Ambler Realty Co.*, 272 U.S. 365 (1926), the Court concluded that a zoning ordinance passed constitutional muster under the equal protection clause if its classifications were not "wholly arbitrary." *Berman* v. *Parker*, 348 U.S. 26 (1954), established the proposition that zoning laws may properly be used, as in this instance, to promote "family values, youth values, and the blessings of quiet seclusion, and clean air. . . ." The challenged zoning ordinance rationally classifies families when measured against its purpose. "It is said, however, that if two unmarried people can constitute a 'family,' there is no reason why three or four may not. But every line drawn by a legislature leaves some out that might well have been included. That exercise of discretion, however, is a legislative not a judicial function."

Finding that the challenged ordinance was not intended to discriminate against transients, unmarried couples, or any other group of persons, the Court rejected the contention that it violated constitutional rights of travel, association, or privacy.

Lehman v. City of Shaker Heights, 418 U.S. 298 (1974)

Facts: A city rapid transit system had a policy of refusing to accept political advertising for car cards on its vehicles but of accepting commercial and other types of advertising. A candidate for state office whose political advertising was refused brought suit claiming that the city's policy violated the First Amendment by discriminating against political speech.

Question: Does a city which operates a public rapid transit system and sells advertising space for car cards on its vehicles violate the First Amendment if it refuses to accept political advertising but generally accepts other types of advertising?

Decision: No. Opinion by Justice Blackmun. Vote: 5–4, Brennan, Stewart, Marshall, and Powell dissenting.

Reasons: The Court reasoned that "[a]lthough American constitutional jurisprudence, in the light of the First Amendment, has been jealous to preserve access to public places for purposes of free speech, the nature of the forum and the conflicting interests involved have remained important in determining the degree of protection afforded by the Amendment to the speech in question." In this case, the city's rapid transit system is a commercial venture and

> has discretion to develop and make reasonable choices concerning the type of advertising that may be displayed in its vehicles. . . . Revenue earned from long-term commercial advertising could be jeopardized by a requirement that short-term candidacy or issue-oriented advertisements be displayed on car cards. Users would be subjected to the blare of political propaganda. There could be lurking doubts about favoritism, and sticky administrative problems might arise in parcelling out limited space to eager politicians. In these circumstances, the managerial decision to limit car card space to innocuous and less controversial commercial and service oriented advertising does not rise to the dignity of a First Amendment violation.

Scheuer v. Rhodes, 416 U.S. 232 (1974)

Facts: The personal representatives of the estates of students who were killed during the May 1970 turmoil at Kent State University brought suit to recover damages under 42 U.S. Code, 1983, against the governor of Ohio, various officers and enlisted members of the Ohio National Guard and the president of Kent State University. Section 1983 authorizes a damage suit against "[e]very person who, under color of [state law]" deprives another of his constitutional rights. The complaints alleged that the defendants, acting under color of state law, willfully and recklessly deprived the students of their lives and rights without due process of law. The federal district court dismissed the complaints on the ground that they in effect alleged claims against the state of Ohio and thus were barred by the Eleventh Amendment. (The Eleventh Amendment bars federal courts from entertaining suits by a private citizen against a state without the state's consent.) The court of appeals affirmed on that ground and on the alternative ground that executive officials were absolutely immune from suit under section 1983.

Question: Were the complaints properly dismissed?

Decision: No. Opinion by Chief Justice Burger. Vote: 8–0, Douglas did not participate.

Reasons: The Eleventh Amendment bars damage suits by private citizens only when payment from a state's treasury is sought. The complaints in this case seek to impose personal liability on the named defendants and thus are not barred by the Eleventh Amendment.

Neither do the defendants enjoy an absolute immunity from suit under section 1983 which literally applies to "[e]very person." Earlier Supreme Court decisions have concluded that Congress did not intend section 1983 to abolish the absolute common-law immunity from suit that state judges and legislators enjoy when acting within their official capacities, but that state executive officers could claim no comparable immunity. However,

> in varying scope, a qualified immunity is available to officers of the executive branch of Government [under section 1983], the variation dependent upon the scope of discretion and responsibilities of the office and all the circumstances as they reasonably appeared at the time of the action on which liability is sought to be based. It is the existence of reasonable grounds for the belief formed at the time and in light of all the circumstances, coupled with good faith belief, that affords a basis for qualified immunity of executive officers for acts performed in the course of official conduct.

The Court thus concluded that the complaints were improperly dismissed because the plaintiffs would be entitled to recover damages under section 1983 if they could prove their allegations that the defendants acted in bad faith and outside the scope of their official duties in depriving the deceased students of constitutional rights.

Spence v. Washington, 418 U.S. 405 (1974)

Facts: For displaying from his apartment window, a United States flag upside down and bearing a large peace symbol, Spence was convicted of violating a Washington state statute prohibiting the exhibition of a flag to which are attached figures, symbols, or other extraneous material. Spence unsuccessfully claimed that because his purpose in affixing the peace symbol to the flag was to express his belief that America stood for peace, prohibition of that action violated his First Amendment right of free speech.

Question: Was Spence's conviction unconstitutional under the First Amendment?

Decision: Yes. Per curiam opinion. Vote: 6–3, Burger, White, and Rehnquist dissenting.

Reasons: The flag in this case was privately owned. It was displayed on private property, and its display created no risk of breach of the peace. The purpose of the questioned display was to "convey a particularized message . . . and in the . . . circumstances the likelihood was great that the message would be understood by those who viewed it." Accordingly, it is clear that Spence was prosecuted for expressing an idea through an action. The state contends that the conviction should be upheld because of the state interest "in preserving the national flag as an unalloyed symbol of our country. . . . Presumably, this interest might be seen as an effort to prevent the appropriation of a revered national symbol by an individual, interest group, or enterprise where there was a risk that association of the symbol with a particular product or viewpoint might be taken erroneously as evidence of governmental endorsement." But even assuming this to be a valid state interest, it was not advanced by Spence's prosecution.

> There was no risk that [Spence's] acts would mislead viewers into assuming that the Government endorsed his viewpoint. . . . [H]is message was direct, likely to be understood, and within the contours of the First Amendment. Given the protected character of his expression and in light of the fact that no interest the State may have in preserving the physical integrity of a privately-owned flag was significantly impaired on these facts, the conviction must be invalidated.

Allee v. Medrano, 416 U.S. 802 (1974)

Facts: A union committee and certain individuals (hereinafter collectively referred to as union supporters) who attempted from June

1966 to June 1967 to unionize farmworkers and persuade them to support or to join a strike in Texas were harassed, intimidated, and physically abused by Texas state and local law enforcement officers. In July 1967, a state court issued a temporary injunction against the union supporters proscribing their picketing on or near property owned by a large farm involved in the dispute. The supporters then brought a civil rights action under 42 U.S. Code, 1983 and 1985 attacking the constitutionality of five Texas statutes relating to breach of the peace and mass picketing. Additionally, they alleged that state and local law enforcement officials had conspired to violate their First and Fourteenth Amendment rights by unlawfully arresting, detaining and confining them without due process and without legal justification, and by unlawfully threatening, harassing, coercing, and physically assaulting them to prevent their exercise of the rights of free speech and assembly.

A three-judge federal district court declared the five challenged state statutes unconstitutional and enjoined their enforcement. (Under 28 U.S. Code, 2281 a three-judge federal district court must be convened in a suit seeking to enjoin enforcement of a state statute on the ground that it is unconstitutional.) The court also enjoined state and local law enforcement officials from using their authority as peace officers to arrest, stop, disperse, or imprison the union supporters, or otherwise interfere with their organizational efforts, without "adequate cause."

On direct appeal to the Supreme Court under 28 U.S. Code, 1253, the defendants contended that (1) the 1967 state court injunction ended the strike, thereby rendering the controversy at issue moot, (2) no irreparable injury was proven to justify the injunction against state and local law enforcement officials, and (3) the district court should have abstained from determining the constitutionality of the five challenged Texas statutes.

Question: Was the three-judge district court decision proper?

Decision: Yes, with the reservation that the Court's holdings that certain state statutes are unconstitutional must be modified. Opinion by Justice Douglas. Vote: 5–3, Burger, White, and Rehnquist dissenting in part. Powell did not participate.

Reasons: Regarding the mootness issue, the state court's temporary injunction proscribed picketing on and near the premises of only one of the major employers in the area in which several incidents occurred. Additionally, no permanent injunction against picketing was ever issued. The state court injunction thus clearly did not settle the issues involved in this lawsuit. The fact that the union supporters temporarily abandoned their organizational and strike efforts did not render the case moot. The union remains "very much a live organization and its goal continues to be the unionization of farm workers." "[T]he very purpose of the suit was to seek protection of the federal court so that the efforts at unionization could be renewed. . . . The essential controversy is therefore . . . very much alive."

With regard to the injunction against the state and local law enforcement authorities, the necessity of showing irreparable injury was clearly shown. The union supporters

> were placed in fear of exercising their constitutionally protected rights of free expression, assembly, and association. Potential supporters of their cause were placed in fear of lending their support. If they were to be able to regain those rights and continue furthering their cause by constitutional means, they required protection from [the law enforcement officers'] concerted conduct. No remedy at law would be adequate to provide such protection.

With regard to the abstention issue, the record fails to disclose whether there were pending state prosecutions under the five challenged statutes at the time the district court enjoined their enforcement. Three of these statutes have been superseded.

> If there are no pending prosecutions *under these superseded statutes*, the District Court should vacate both the declaratory and injunctive relief as to them. If there are pending prosecutions remaining against any of the [union supporters], then the District Court should make findings as to whether these particular prosecutions were brought in bad faith, with no genuine expectation of conviction. If it so finds, the court will enter an appropriate decree which this Court may ultimately review, both as to the propriety of federal court intervention in the circumstances of the case, and as to the merits of any holding striking down the state statutes.

As to the two remaining statutes, the Court ruled that "[i]f there are pending prosecutions then the District Court should determine whether they were brought in bad faith, for the purpose of harassing [union supporters] and deterring the exercise of First Amendment rights, so that allowing the prosecutions to proceed will result in irreparable injury to the [supporters]." If such a determination is made, injunctive relief would be proper. If there are no pending prosecutions and only declaratory relief against threatened prosecutions is sought, then *Steffel* v. *Thompson*, 415 U.S. 452 (1974), would permit granting the requested relief without proof of bad faith enforcement of the challenged statutes or other special circumstances. Accordingly, the Court vacated the district court's judgment as to the five challenged statutes and remanded the case for further proceedings.

Elections

The Court's most important decisions concerning elections should have the effect of strengthening the two-party system. In recent years, the number of minor party or independent candidates has multiplied as the power of the two major parties has declined. Approximately one-third of the American voters are now registered as independents. In two major cases, the Court upheld the constitutionality of a variety of election law provisions designed to restrict the ability of minor and independent candidates to gain access to the ballot. Generally speaking, the Court reasoned that the restrictions were justified by the state interest in protecting the integrity of the nominating process of political parties and in avoiding voter confusion that would be caused by placing numerous candidates on the ballot. The restrictions upheld included provisions that (1) require minor party or independent candidates to gather a certain number of signatures during a limited time to qualify for the ballot, and (2) forbid ballot position to an independent candidate if he voted in the preceding party primary elections or was affiliated with a major political party at any time within one year prior to the preceding primary election.

The Court, however, held other restrictions on candidates and voters to be unconstitutional. In one case the Court struck down a state statute requiring a filing fee of several hundred dollars as a qualification for appearing on the ballot. This decision followed naturally from the Court's earlier ruling in *Bullock* v. *Carter*, 405 U.S. 134 (1972), that substantial filing fees could not be justified by the state's interest in limiting the ballot to serious candidates. That interest, the Court noted, can be served by requiring that petitions be signed by a certain minimum number of qualified voters as a condition for a candidate to appear on the ballot. In another case, the Court rejected the claim that prevention of party "raiding" in primaries justified prohibiting a person from voting in the primary election of a political party if he had voted in the primary of any other party within the preceding twenty-three months. In declaring the prohibition unconstitutional, the Court seemed to depart from the spirit of its decision last term in *Rosario* v. *Rockefeller*, 410 U.S. 752 (1973). There the Court gave great weight to the state interest in inhibiting party "raiding" whereby voters in sympathy with one party designate themselves as voters of another party in order to influence or determine the results of the other party's primary.

The Court's recent decisions concerning election law restrictions seem to lack any doctrinal consistency and seem to justify Justice White's observation in *Storer* v. *Brown*, 415 U.S. 724 (1974), that what the Court will do in any case is "very difficult to predict with great assurance."

American Party of Texas v. *White*, 415 U.S. 767 (1974)

Facts: Minority political parties and their candidates, qualified voters supporting minority party candidates, and independent unaffiliated candidates brought several separate lawsuits challenging the constitutionality of various provisions of the Texas Election Code which restricted the right of minority party and independent candidates from appearing on the general election ballot. The Texas Election Code requires a minor party (defined as a party whose candidate polled less than 2 percent of the total vote cast for governor in the last general election) to hold precinct nominating conventions in order to qualify for the ballot. If the number of qualified voters at those conventions number 1 percent or more of the total vote cast for governor at the prior election, the minor party qualifies for the ballot. Ballot qualification is also secured if within 55 days of the precinct convention the minor party obtains petitions signed by sufficient numbers of qualified voters which when combined with the convention participants reaches the requisite 1 percent figure. Independent candidates may qualify for the ballot under the Election Code if within a 30-day period signatures of qualified voters are gathered in number ranging from 1 to 5 percent of the total votes cast in the prior gubernatorial election depending on the office sought. However, in no event is the number of required signatures to exceed five hundred for candidates seeking "district office." Voters who had participated in another party's nominating process were disqualified from signing minor party or independent candidate petitions. Additionally, the state printed only the names of the Democratic and Republican candidates on absentee ballots. The thrust of the constitutional claims was that the Texas Election Code restrictions on minor party and independent candidate access to the ballot violated First Amendment rights of free speech and association and discriminated against new or small political parties in violation of the equal protection clause.

Question: Are the challenged Texas Election Code provisions constitutional?

Decision: All the provisions are constitutional, except for the practice of excluding minor party candidates from the absentee ballot. Opinion by Justice White. Vote: 8–1, Douglas dissenting in part.

Reasons: "[W]hether the qualifications for ballot position are viewed as substantial burdens on the right to associate or as discriminations against parties not polling 2 percent of the last election vote, their validity depend upon whether they are necessary to further compelling state interests. . . ." With regard to the claims asserted by minor parties, the Court stated that states have a compelling interest in regulating the number of candidates on the ballot to avoid undue voter confusion. In light of that vital state interest, the requirement that minor parties demonstrate support from electors equal in number to 1 percent of the vote for governor at the last election in order to qualify for the ballot is neither unreasonable nor unconstitutional. Demonstration of this support is not impractical. Minor parties are entitled to compete for voter support before major party primary elections and to seek participants at its convention on primary day. If the number of participants falls short of the 1 percent figure, ballot position may be secured by obtaining sufficient signatures within a 55-day period beginning after the primary and ending 120 days prior to the general election.

The state interest in protecting the integrity of the party nominating process justifies the disqualification of "those who have voted at a party primary from signing petitions for another party seeking ballot position for its candidates for the same offices." With regard to the 55-day period for circulating supplemental petitions to reach the 1 percent figure, the Court upheld its constitutionality reasoning that the period was not unduly short and that the requisite signatures could be obtained if one hundred canvassers secured only four each day. The Court also rejected the contention that a provision requiring notarization of all signatures evidencing support for a minor party was unconstitutionally burdensome.

With regard to the independent candidate claims, the Court stated that "[d]emanding signatures equal in number [up] to . . . five percent of the vote in the last election [as a condition to appear on the general election ballot] is not invalid on its face" under *Jenness* v. *Fortson,* 403 U.S. 431 (1971). There the Court upheld a Georgia statute requiring a minor party candidate to file a nominating petition as a condition for access to the general election ballot, which contained signatures of 5 percent of the voters registered at the last general election in the area the candidate sought to represent. In this case, the Court reasoned that the 500-signature limit for district office candidates and the failure of the record to provide any factual basis for the claim that the 5 percent figure was unduly burdensome required rejection of the assertion that independent candidates were unconstitutionally restricted under the Election Code in gaining access to the ballot.

The Court rejected the equal protection challenges of both minor parties and independent candidates. Those claims rested largely upon the fact that the Election Code permitted major parties to gain ballot access automatically by holding primary elections financed by state revenues. The costs of circulating petitions and of holding minor party conventions were not financed from the state treasury. The Court found no invidious discrimination in the different treatment accorded a major party. A major party possesses sufficient prima facie electoral support, the Court concluded, to justify automatic ballot access. The relatively large expense in conducting primary elections compared to the costs of circulating petitions and holding minor party conventions, the Court reasoned, justified state financial support for the former but not the latter.

The Court held that the state's practice of printing only the names of Republican and Democratic candidates on the absentee ballot but not those of other candidates who qualified for the general ballot was invidiously discriminatory in violation of the equal protection clause. The issue of whether absentee ballots must also include names of candidates not qualifying for the general ballot was remanded for consideration in light of *O'Brien* v. *Skinner*, 414 U.S. 524 (1974). From that case, "it is plain that permitting absentee voting by some classes of voters and denying the privilege to other classes of otherwise qualified voters in similar circumstances, without affording a comparable alternative means to vote, is an arbitrary discrimination violative of the Equal Protection Clause."

Storer v. *Brown*, 415 U.S. 724 (1974)

Facts: The California Election Code forbids ballot position to an independent candidate for elective public office if he voted in the preceding party primary elections, or if he had a registered affiliation with a qualified political party at any time within one year prior to the preceding primary election. To secure a ballot position, an independent candidate must file nomination papers signed by 5 to 6 percent of the entire vote cast in the preceding general election in the area which the candidate seeks to represent. These signatures must be obtained during a 24-day period following the primary and ending 60 days prior to the general election, and from persons who have not voted at the primary election. The constitutionality of these provisions was challenged on the grounds that they impinged upon First Amendment rights of political association and invidiously discriminated against independent candidates in violation of the equal protection clause.

Question: Are the challenged California Election Code provisions constitutional?

Decision: The restrictions on ballot access to independent candidates who recently changed party preferences are constitutional. Further proceedings must take place in district court to determine whether the signature requirements place an unconstitutional burden on independent candidates' access to the ballot. Opinion by Justice White. Vote: 6–3, Douglas, Brennan, and Marshall dissenting.

Reasons: The Court observed that the rule it had fashioned

> to pass on constitutional challenges to specific provisions of election laws provides no litmus-paper test for separating those restrictions that are valid from those that are invidious under the Equal Protection Clause. . . . Decision in this context, as in others, is very much a "matter of degree" . . . very much a matter of "consider[ing] the facts and circumstances behind the law, the interest which the State claims to be protecting, and the interest of those who are disadvantaged by the classification." . . . What the result of this process will be in any specific case may be very difficult to predict with great assurance.

The requirement that an independent candidate have no affiliation with a political party for a year before the primary elections reflects a strong state interest in maintaining the integrity of the nomination process. The direct party primary in California is intended to settle intraparty feuds so that the general election ballot can be reserved for major political contestants. The challenged provisions regarding disentanglement from political parties "protect[s] the direct primary process by refusing to recognize independent candidates who do not make early plans to leave a party and take the alternate course to the ballot. It works against independent candidacies prompted by short-range political goals, pique, or personal quarrel. It is also a substantial barrier to a party fielding an 'independent' candidate to capture and bleed off votes in the general election that might well go to another party." The Court noted that the challenged provisions required an independent candidate to anticipate his candidacy one year in advance of his election campaign. Nevertheless, the state interest in protecting the integrity of the nominating process justified that restriction on independent candidates, at least as applied in this case where the litigants had disaffiliated with a party no more than six months prior to the primary elections.

Regarding the 5 to 6 percent signature requirements, the Court concluded that in order "to assess realistically whether the law imposes excessively burdensome requirements upon independent candidates it is necessary to know other critical facts which do not appear from the evidentiary record in this case." The Court stated that the requirement that candidates gather signatures equal to 5 percent of the total vote cast in the last general election was not excessive on its face. However, because California law disqualified all registered voters who voted in the primary from signing an independent candidate's petition, it was likely that signatures would have to be gathered from substantially more than 5 percent of the eligible pool. The Court directed the district court to determine "whether the available pool is so diminished in size by the disqualification of those who voted in the primary that the . . . signature requirement, to be satisfied in 24 days, is too great a burden on the independent candidate. . . ." The Court indicated that if the required signatures approached 10 percent of the eligible pool of voters, the requirement that those signatures be collected within 24 days following the primary elections would be unconstitutional, because it was not necessary to serve the state's compelling interest in keeping the names of frivolous candidates off the ballot.

Lubin v. Panish, 415 U.S. 709 (1974)

Facts: A California statute requires that a candidate pay a $700 filing fee in order to be placed on the ballot in the primary election for nomination to the office of county supervisor. No alternative method for placement on the ballot is provided. The constitutionality of the statute was challenged on the ground that it deprived indigents of equal protection and First Amendment rights of free speech and association.

Question: Is the California filing fee statute unconstitutional?

Decision: Yes. Opinion by Chief Justice Burger. Vote: 9–0.

Reasons: The state contends that the statutory fee is "necessary to keep the ballot from being overwhelmed with frivolous or otherwise nonserious candidates. . . ." In *Bullock* v. *Carter*, 405 U.S. 134 (1972), the Court "recognized that the State's interest in keeping its ballots within manageable, understandable limits is of the highest order. . . . This legitimate state interest, however, must be achieved by a means that does not unfairly or unnecessarily burden either a minority party's or an individual candidate's equally important interest in the continued availability of political opportunity. The interests involved are not merely those of parties or individual candidates; the voters can assert their preferences only through candidates or parties or both and it is this broad interest that must be weighed in the balance." The Court reasoned in this case that payment of a filing fee did not accurately measure the seriousness of a candidacy because a wealthy candidate with no support could secure a place on the ballot, whereas a serious though indigent candidate would be excluded. The Court thus held that the challenged filing fee statute was unconstitutional because not "reasonably necessary" to secure the state's legitimate interest in excluding frivolous candidates from the ballot. The Court noted, however, that "States may . . . impose on minor political parties the precondition of demonstrating the existence [of] some reasonable quantum of voter support by requiring such parties to file petitions for a place on the ballot signed by a percentage of those who voted in a prior election." However, the Court strongly suggested that permitting indigent candidates to receive write-in votes without payment of the filing fee would not satisfy the constitutional defect in the challenged California filing fee system.

Kusper v. Pontikes, 414 U.S. 51 (1973)

Facts: An Illinois voter challenged the constitutionality of a provision in the Illinois Election Code that prohibited a person from voting in the primary election of a political party if he had voted in the primary of any other party within the preceding twenty-three months. The voter successfully claimed before a three-judge federal court that the restriction on voting abridged her freedom to associate with the political party of her choice. The state contended that the provision was needed to prevent party "raiding" in primaries.

Question: Does the challenged Illinois Election Code provision violate the First Amendment's guarantee of free association?

Decision: Yes. Opinion by Justice Stewart. Vote: 7–2, Blackmun and Rehnquist dissenting.

Reasons: Finding that the state court interpretation of the challenged state statute was clear, the Court first rejected the contention that the three-judge federal district court should have abstained from its adjudication.

Turning to the merits, the Court concluded that a state may not significantly encroach upon political associational freedom if it has a less drastic way available to satisfy its legitimate interests. The Court reasoned that the challenged provision "locks" voters into a preexisting party affiliation from one primary to the next, and the only way to break the "lock" is to forego voting in any primary for a period of almost two years. That device "conspicuously infringes upon basic constitutional liberty." The Illinois state interest in preventing party raiding can be accomplished by less drastic restrictions upon the right to vote, through adoption of a statute similar to the one challenged in *Rosario* v. *Rockefeller*, 410 U.S. 752 (1973). There the Court upheld a New York antiraiding statute that required voters wishing to vote in a different party primary every year to declare their appropriate party allegiance thirty days before the preceding general election. "The New York law did not have the consequence of 'locking' a voter into an unwanted party affiliation from one election to the next. . . ."

Communist Party of Indiana v. *Whitcomb*, 414 U.S. 441 (1974)

Facts: Presidential and vice presidential candidates of the Communist party of Indiana were refused a place on Indiana's national ballot because officers of that party had failed to file an affidavit, as required by Indiana law, stating that the Communist party did not "advocate the overthrow of local, state or national government by force or violence. . . ." The candidates brought suit contending that the required loyalty oath was unconstitutional under the First Amendment because it excluded from the ballot persons advocating abstract doctrine as well as advocacy of action.

Question: Is the challenged Indiana loyalty oath requirement invalid under the First Amendment because it excludes from the ballot persons who advocate the overthrow of the Government as an abstract doctrine?

Decision: Yes. Opinion by Justice Brennan. Vote: 9–0.

Reasons: Prior Supreme Court cases have clearly established the constitutional principle that the First Amendment forbids a state from either proscribing or otherwise regulating the advocacy of the use of force or of law violation except where such advocacy is directed to inciting or producing imminent lawless action and is likely to incite or produce such action. Under that principle, Indiana's refusal to place on the ballot those advocating mere abstract doctrine violates the First Amendment.

Federal Courts and Procedure

The caseload of federal courts has increased dramatically at all levels since 1960. In that year, the number of cases commenced in federal district courts was approximately 89,000, the number of appeals filed in federal courts of appeals was 3,900, and the number of cases docketed in the Supreme Court was 2,296. By 1974, the comparable figures were 143,000 for federal district courts, 16,400 for federal courts of appeals, and 4,460 for the Supreme Court. In percentage terms, the number of cases filed in the district courts, the courts of appeals, and the Supreme Court since 1960 has increased by approximately 63 percent, 400 percent, and 100 percent, respectively.

The view that the federal judiciary is generally "overworked" may have been a factor this term in Supreme Court decisions dealing with standing, class actions, and federal jurisdiction—decisions which on balance tended to create obstacles to suing in federal court. With regard to standing, the Court ruled that (1) a taxpayer lacks standing to challenge the constitutionality of a statute that permits the CIA to keep its expenditures secret, (2) taxpayers and citizens both lack standing to challenge whether the Constitution permits congressmen to hold reserve commissions in the armed forces, and (3) a shareholder lacks standing to challenge illegalities that occurred before he purchased his shares. The Court recognized that its decisions may leave only the political process to remedy certain constitutional violations.

In a decision that will slow the growing number of consumer class action suits, a unanimous Court ruled that plaintiffs bringing such suits must bear the cost of notifying each member of the class. The class in question had some six million members, and notification of each one would have cost a total of $225 thousand. In a related decision concerning class actions brought under state law, the Court ruled that federal courts generally lack jurisdiction to hear such suits unless each member of the class has in excess of $10 thousand in controversy.

The Court's decisions, however, did not all have the effect of decreasing the caseload of the federal judiciary. It held that the termination of a labor dispute did not moot the issue of whether strikers could receive welfare benefits. Having expressed in *Younger* v. *Harris*,

401 U.S. 37 (1971), and subsequent cases an inclination to avoid conflict with state judicial proceedings, the Court retreated somewhat from the spirit of those decisions and held that federal courts may declare a state criminal statute unconstitutional without having proof that state authorities are threatening prosecution under it in bad faith. In another case, the Court held that a federal court had "pendent jurisdiction" to adjudicate a state law claim that was joined with a constitutional claim in a single lawsuit.

At least partially responsible for the backlog of civil cases in federal courts is the Seventh Amendment right to a jury trial in suits at common law. Last term, the Court upheld the constitutionality of six-man jury trials in *Colgrove* v. *Battin*, 413 U.S. 149 (1973). Nevertheless, civil jury trials in general take more time and judicial resources than do judge trials. Arguing that the Seventh amendment is obsolete, some have urged its repeal. Until it is repealed, however, civil jury trials and Seventh Amendment issues will continue to burden the federal judiciary. This term, the Court held that tenants have a constitutional right to jury trial in eviction suits. The Court also ruled that a constitutional right to trial by jury attaches to damage suits brought under the 1968 Civil Rights Act.

United States v. Richardson, 418 U.S. 166 (1974)

Facts: A federal taxpayer brought suit in federal district court claiming that the provision in the Central Intelligence Agency Act permitting the agency to account for its expenditures "solely on the certificate of the Director. . . ." violated Article I, section 9, clause 7 of the Constitution. That clause provides in part that "a regular statement of account of the receipts and expenditures of all public money shall be published from time to time." The taxpayer alleged he was injured by his inability to obtain a document setting forth the expenditures and receipts of the Central Intelligence Agency. The district court dismissed the suit on the ground, *inter alia*, that the taxpayer lacked standing. The court of appeals reversed, holding that the taxpayer had standing under the standards enunciated in *Flast* v. *Cohen*, 392 U.S. 83 (1968). There the Court concluded that a federal taxpayer has standing to challenge the constitutionality of a federal statute if he alleges (1) a "logical link" between his status as a taxpayer and the challenged legislative enactment, that is, an attack on legislation enacted under the taxing and spending clause of Article I, section 8 of the Constitution, and (2) a "nexus" between his status and a specific constitutional limitation imposed on the taxing and spending power.

Question: Did the federal taxpayer have standing to maintain this suit?

Decision: No. Opinion by Chief Justice Burger. Vote: 5–4, Douglas, Brennan, Stewart, and Marshall dissenting.

Reasons: In this case, the taxpayer is challenging statutes regulating the Central Intelligence Agency with regard to accounting and reporting requirements. He does not allege that appropriated funds are being spent in violation of a specific constitutional limitation upon the spending power. "Rather, he asks the courts to compel the Government to give him information on precisely how the CIA spends its funds." Accordingly, the taxpayer's claims do not "meet the standards for taxpayer standing set forth in *Flast*" which require allegations that the challenged enactment exceeds specific constitutional limitations imposed on the taxing and spending power.

The Court also concluded that the taxpayer lacked standing to sue because he failed to allege that the operation of the challenged statute was causing him some particular concrete injury. The Court concluded that the taxpayer's grievance was "plainly undifferentiated and 'common to all members of the public.' " Noting that its decision might preclude anyone from litigating the substantive issue raised by the taxpayer's suit, the Court suggested that the issue be settled through the operation of the political process rather than through the judicial process.

> In a very real sense, the absence of any particular individual or class to litigate these claims gives support to the argument that the subject matter is committed to the surveillance of Congress, and ultimately to the political process. Any other conclusion would mean that the Founding Fathers intended to set up something in the nature of an Athenian democracy or a New England town meeting to oversee the conduct of the National Government by means of lawsuits in federal courts. . . . Slow, cumbersome and unresponsive though the traditional electoral process may be thought at times, our system provides for changing members of the political branches when dissatisfied citizens convince a sufficient number of their fellow electors that elected representatives are delinquent in performing duties committed to them.

Schlesinger v. Reservists Committee to Stop the War, 418 U.S. 208 (1974)

Facts: An association of present and former members of the

Armed Forces Reserve and five association members brought a class action in federal district court on behalf, *inter alia*, of all United States citizens and taxpayers. Naming the secretary of defense and three service secretaries as defendants, the Reserve association alleged that Article I, section 6, clause 2 of the Constitution (the incompatibility clause) renders a member of Congress ineligible to hold a commission in the Armed Forces Reserve during his continuance in office. That clause provides that "no person holding any office under the United States shall be a Member of either House during his continuance in office."

The Reserve association sought (1) an order in the nature of mandamus directed to the defendants requiring them to strike from the rolls of the Reserves all members of Congress, to discharge any member of the Reserves who subsequently became a member of Congress, and to seek to reclaim from members and former members of Congress any Reserve pay such members received while serving in Congress, (2) a permanent injunction preventing the defendants from placing on the rolls of the Reserves any member of Congress, and (3) a declaration that membership in the Reserves is an office under the United States prohibited to members of Congress by the incompatibility clause. The complaint alleged that members of Congress who hold a position in the Reserves cause injury to citizens and taxpayers because they might (1) be unduly influenced by the executive, and (2) have inconsistent Reserve and congressional obligations. The district court held that the Reserve association had standing to sue as citizens, but not as taxpayers, and on the merits held that the incompatibility clause renders a member of Congress ineligible, during his continuance in office, from holding a Reserve "commission." The court of appeals affirmed.

Question: Did the Reserve association have standing either as citizens or as federal taxpayers to bring this claim?

Decision: No. Opinion by Chief Justice Burger. Vote: 6–3, Douglas, Brennan, and Marshall dissenting.

Reasons: In *Baker* v. *Carr*, 369 U.S. 186 (1962), the Court stated that the gist of the inquiry in determining when a complaining party has standing is whether he alleges "such a personal stake in the outcome of the controversy as to insure that concrete adverseness which sharpens the presentation of issues upon which the Court so largely depends for illumination of difficult constitutional questions." A party must allege some concrete injury, either actual or threatened, in order to have a sufficient personal stake in the outcome of a suit to have standing. "To permit a complainant who has no concrete injury to require a court to rule on important constitutional issues in the abstract would create the potential for abuse of the judicial process, distort the role of the Judiciary in its relationship to the Executive and the Legislature and open the Judiciary to an arguable charge of providing 'government by injunction.' "

In this case, the Reserve association, as a group of citizens, has alleged only abstract and speculative, as opposed to concrete, injury. The complaint "reveals that it is nothing more than a matter of speculation whether the claimed nonobservance of [the incompatibility] Clause deprives citizens of the faithful discharge of the legislative duties of Reservist Members of Congress. And that claimed nonobservance, standing alone, would adversely affect only the generalized interest of all citizens in constitutional governance, and that is an abstract injury." Accordingly, the association lacked standing as a citizen to bring this suit because no concrete injury was alleged.

The Court also concluded that the Reserve association lacked standing as a taxpayer to sue under the standards established in *Flast* v. *Cohen*, 392 U.S. 83 (1968). (See *United States* v. *Richardson*, 418 U.S. 166 (1974) for a discussion of the *Flast* standards.) The Court reasoned that since the complaint did not challenge a statute enacted pursuant to the taxing and spending clause of Article I, section 8, but rather the action of the executive branch in permitting members of Congress to maintain their Reserve status, the association's standing as a taxpaying organization failed under *Flast*.

Bangor Punta Operations, Inc. v. Bangor & Aroostook R.R. Co., 417 U.S. 703 (1974)

Facts: In 1964, the Bangor Punta Corporation acquired 98.3 percent of the stock of the Bangor & Aroostook Railroad Company. In 1969, Bangor Punta sold its Bangor & Aroostook stock to Amoskeag Company, which assumed control of the railroad and later acquired additional shares to gain ownership of more than 99 percent of all the outstanding stock. In 1971, Bangor & Aroostook sued Bangor Punta in federal district court alleging various acts of corporate mismanagement during the period from 1960 through 1967 and seeking to recover damages under federal antitrust and securities laws and under certain laws of the state of Maine. The district court reasoned that Amoskeag, which owned over 99 percent of the Bangor & Aroostook stock, would be the actual beneficiary of any recovery and thus was the true plaintiff in the suit.

Concluding that the suit was tantamount to a shareholder's derivative action, the district court dismissed it on the ground that under rule 23.1(b)(1) of the Federal Rules of Civil Procedure and Maine state law a stockholder bringing such a suit must have been a stockholder at the time of the alleged wrongdoing. (Amoskeag, the shareholder of Bangor & Aroostook, owned no shares of that company at the time it was allegedly damaged by Bangor Punta.)

The court of appeals reversed the district court's ruling. It reasoned that railroads are "quasi-public" corporations and that any Bangor & Aroostook recovery would benefit the public. The court of appeals suggested that the district court devise a method to ensure that any recovery be used to improve railroad services rather than to pay dividends to Amoskeag. Stating that the suit would provide a needed deterrent to mismanagement of the nation's railroads, the court of appeals concluded that Bangor & Aroostook should be granted standing as a plaintiff.

Question: Did the court of appeals err in concluding that Bangor & Aroostook should be permitted to bring suit against Bangor Punta?

Decision: Yes. Opinion by Justice Powell. Vote: 5–4, Marshall, Douglas, Brennan, and White dissenting.

Reasons: The resolution of whether Bangor & Aroostook should be permitted to maintain its federal claims against Bangor Punta "depends upon the applicability of the settled principle of equity that a shareholder may not complain of acts of corporate mismanagement if he acquired his shares from those who participated or acquiesced in the allegedly wrongful transactions." The basic reasoning behind that principle is to prevent shareholders from receiving a "windfall" despite "the fact that they received all that they bargained for." In this case, Amoskeag would be the principal beneficiary of any recovery by Bangor & Aroostook against Bangor Punta. Yet Amoskeag does not contend that it received less than full value for its money in purchasing Bangor & Aroostook stock after the acts of alleged wrongdoing. Accordingly, federal principles of equity preclude Amoskeag, through the guise of suing in the name of Bangor & Aroostook, to maintain its federal claims against Bangor Punta. Because Maine law adheres to the same principles of equity, the state law claims must also be dismissed.

The Court rejected the contention that Bangor & Aroostook should be permitted to maintain the suit in order to deter mismanagement of railroads. That rationale, the Court concluded, logically would permit any plaintiff to sue without alleging any particular injury to, or violation of a legal duty toward, himself.

Eisen v. Carlisle & Jacquelin, 417 U.S. 156 (1974)

Facts: A purchaser of odd-lot shares filed a class action suit in federal district court on behalf of himself and all other odd-lot traders on the New York Stock Exchange (NYSE) during the period 1962–1966 alleging violations of the antitrust laws by brokerage firms and of the securities laws by the exchange. (Odd-lots are shares traded in lots of less than one hundred.) The purchaser's individual stake in the damages award sought was only seventy dollars. Rule 23(a) of the Federal Rules of Civil Procedure sets forth four prerequisites to the maintenance of any suit as a class action: "(1) the class is so numerous that joinder of all members is impracticable, (2) there are questions of law or fact common to the class, (3) the claims or defenses of the representative parties are typical of the claims or defenses of the class, and (4) the representative parties will fairly and adequately protect the interests of the class." In addition to meeting these four requirements, a suit may proceed as a class action only if it also satisfies one of three subdivisions of rule 23(b). Subdivision (3) of that rule provides that the court must find "that the questions of law or fact common to the members of the class predominate over any questions affecting only individual members, and that a class action is superior to other available methods for the fair and efficient adjudication of the controversy." In making the findings required under subdivision (3), a court is directed to consider "the difficulties likely to be encountered in the management of a class action." The district court concluded that the suit met the requirements of subdivision (a) and subdivision (b)(3) and thus could be maintained as a class action.

In considering problems of manageability under (b)(3), the district court dealt with problems of the computation of damages, the mechanics of administering this suit as a class action, and the distribution of any eventual recovery. Because the prospective class included some six million members, the court concluded that any damages would be distributed to future odd-lot traders by lowering their commission charges. The need to resort to this expedient of recovery arose from the prohibitively high cost of computing and awarding multitudinous small damage claims on an individual basis.

The district court found that some two-and-a-quarter-million members of the prospective class could be identified by name and address with reasonable effort and that it would cost $225 thousand to send individual notice to all of them. Because of the expense in notifying all such prospective class members, the district court proposed a $21 thousand notification scheme involving individual notice for only a limited number and notice by newspaper for the remainder. The district court then held a preliminary hearing on the merits and determined that the purchaser was "more than likely" to prevail at trial and thus ordered the defendants to pay 90 percent of the cost of notice. (The district court devised this novel procedure because the purchaser clearly would have refused to pay $21 thousand to notify prospective class members when his individual stake in the litigation was only seventy dollars.) On direct review, the court of appeals reversed the district court's decision and ordered the suit dismissed as a class action. It held that rule 23(c)(2) required individual notice to all identifiable class members; that the preliminary hearing on the merits for the purpose of allocating the cost of notice was improper; that the purchaser should bear the entire cost of notice; and that the proposed class action was unmanageable under rule 23(b)(3).

Questions: (1) Did the court of appeals have jurisdiction to review the district court's orders permitting the suit to proceed as a class action and allocating the cost of notice? (2) Must the purchaser bear the entire cost of notifying each individual prospective class member before the suit may proceed as a class action?

Decision: Yes to both questions. Opinion by Justice Powell. Vote: 9–0, Douglas, Brennan, and Marshall dissenting in part.

Reasons: Regarding the question of whether the court of appeals had jurisdiction to review the district court's order, 28 U.S. Code 1291 provides for appellate review only of "final" orders. The requirement of finality is to be given a practical construction. This case is controlled by *Cohen v. Beneficial Loan Corp.*, 337 U.S. 541 (1949). There the Court established the principle that a district court decision is "final" for purposes of section 1291 if it "finally determine[s] claims of right separable from, and collateral to, rights asserted in the action, too important to be denied review and too independent of the cause itself to require that appellate consideration be deferred until the whole case is adjudicated." In this case, the district court's decision on the allocation of notice costs was collateral to the merits of the suit and was too important to be denied review until the whole suit was adjudicated. Accordingly, the decision was "final" under *Cohen* and thus the court of appeals had jurisdiction to review it under section 1291.

With regard to the district court's resolution of the notice problem, it failed to comply with rule 23(c)(2) and erroneously imposed part of the cost of notice on the defendants.

Rule 23(c)(2) provides that, in any class action maintained under subdivision (b)(3), each class member shall be advised that he has the right to exclude himself from the action on request or to enter an appearance through counsel, and further that the judgment, whether favorable or not, will bind all class members not requesting exclusion. To this end, the court is required to direct to class members "the best notice practicable under the circumstances, *including individual notice to all members who can be identified through reasonable effort.*" Rule 23(c)(2) clearly requires that "[i]ndividual notice must be sent to all class members whose names and addresses may be ascertained through reasonable effort." Therefore, the district court erred in failing to require that the two-and-a-quarter-million prospective class members who could be identified by name and address with reasonable effort be individually notified by mail.

The district court also erred in imposing 90 percent of the notice costs on the defendants after conducting a preliminary hearing under rule 23 on the merits. "[N]othing in either the language or history of Rule 23 . . . gives a court any authority to conduct a preliminary inquiry into the merits of a suit in order to determine whether it may be maintained as a class action." Moreover, the plaintiff must initially bear the cost of notice to the class "as part of the ordinary burden of financing his own suit" when its relationship to the defendant, as in this case, is "truly adversarial."

Because the purchaser had stated his refusal to bear the cost of notice to members of the class as defined in the original complaint, the Court remanded the case with instructions to dismiss the class action as so defined. The Court left open the question of whether a class action might properly be maintained on behalf of a smaller group of odd-lot traders.

Zahn v. International Paper Company, 414 U.S. 291 (1973)

Facts: Alleging jurisdiction under 28 U.S.C., 1332(a), a class action suit was brought in federal district court in which only the named class representatives claimed more than $10 thousand in controversy. Section 1332(a) confers jurisdiction upon federal district courts to hear suits between citizens of diverse states only when the "matter in controversy" exceeds $10 thousand. The federal district court refused to permit the suit to proceed as a class action reasoning that section 1332(a) required each member of a class to satisfy the

$10 thousand minimum jurisdictional amount requirement.

Question: Does section 1332(a) forbid the maintenance of a class action unless each class member satisfies the jurisdictional amount requirement?

Decision: Yes. Opinion by Justice White. Vote: 6–3, Brennan, Douglas, and Marshall dissenting.

Reasons: In *Snyder* v. *Harris*, 394 U.S. 332 (1969), the Court held that individual class members could not aggregate their claims in order to satisfy the $10 thousand jurisdictional amount required under section 1332(a). *Snyder* was soundly based upon a longstanding court interpretation of the phrase "matter in controversy" to mean that "each of several plaintiffs asserting separate and distinct claims must satisfy the jurisdictional amount requirement if his claim was to survive a motion to dismiss." The rationale of *Snyder* compels the conclusion that under section 1332(a) any plaintiff failing to satisfy "the jurisdictional amount must be dismissed from the case, even though others allege jurisdictionally sufficient claims." The Court added that this rule would also apply to claims arising under federal law brought under 28 U.S.C., 1331, which, like section 1332, has a $10 thousand jurisdictional amount requirement.

Steffel v. Thompson, 415 U.S. 452 (1974)

Facts: Warned twice to stop handbilling on a shopping center sidewalk and threatened with arrest for criminal trespass, Steffel sued in federal district court claiming that the criminal trespass statute as applied to him was unconstitutional. Seeking declaratory relief, Steffel argued that the challenged statute violated his First and Fourteenth Amendment rights of free speech. Steffel's declaratory judgment claim was ultimately dismissed on the ground that declaratory relief is unavailable to test the constitutionality of a threatened prosecution under a state criminal law in the absence of proof that such threats constitute "bad faith harassment."

Question: Must "bad faith harassment" be proven by a person threatened with prosecution under a state criminal law before he may properly seek a declaration in federal district court that the law is unconstitutional?

Decision: No. Opinion by Justice Brennan. Vote: 9-0.

Reasons: In *Samuels* v. *Mackell*, 401 U.S. 66 (1971), the Court concluded that principles of equity, comity, and federalism would be flouted if a federal court declared unconstitutional a state criminal statute that was the basis of a pending state prosecution against the federal plaintiff.

The Court held in *Samuels* that without bad faith enforcement or other special circumstances, the federal plaintiff should be required to vindicate his constitutional rights in the pending state proceedings. However, where, as here, no state criminal proceedings are pending, considerations of equity, comity, and federalism have little vitality. In such circumstances, federal declaratory relief is not precluded when the federal plaintiff has been threatened with prosecution under an allegedly unconstitutional state statute, even if bad-faith enforcement or other special circumstances have not been demonstrated. To conclude otherwise would deprive federal courts of their central role in enforcing constitutional rights.

Super Tire Engineering Co. v. McCorkle, 416 U.S. 115 (1974)

Facts: New Jersey law permits employees engaged in an economic strike to receive state welfare benefits. New Jersey employers whose plants were struck by union employees brought suit against New Jersey welfare administrators seeking to enjoin them from making state welfare funds available to the strikers and a declaration that to do so would be unconstitutional under the supremacy clause. The theory of the employers' case was that providing state welfare benefits to striking workers interfered with the federal labor policy of free collective bargaining expressed in the National Labor Relations Act. The district court ruled against the employers on the merits, although the strike had terminated at the time of decision. Without reaching the merits, the court of appeals concluded that the case should have been dismissed for mootness because of the strike's termination.

Question: Did the court of appeals err in ordering the suit dismissed for mootness?

Decision: Yes. Opinion by Justice Blackmun. Vote: 5–4, Stewart, Burger, Powell, and Rehnquist dissenting.

Reasons: Whether the employers' request for declaratory relief was mooted by the settlement of the strike depends upon whether there remained "a substantial controversy, between parties having adverse legal interests. . . ." The substantiality requirement is met in this case because "the availability of state welfare assistance for striking workers in New Jersey pervades every work stoppage, affects every existing collective-bargaining agreement, and is a factor lurking in the background of every incipient labor contract. . . . Where . . . state action or its imminence adversely affects the status of private parties, the courts should be available to render appropriate relief and judgments affecting the parties' rights and interests." The Court added that to condition judicial consideration of the issues presented in this case on the existence of an economic strike would frustrate the judicial process because "the great majority of economic strikes do not last long enough for complete judicial review of the controversies they engender."

Hagans v. Lavine, 415 U.S. 528 (1974)

Facts: Recipients of public assistance under the cooperative federal-state Aid to Families with Dependent Children (AFDC) program brought suit in federal district court challenging the constitutionality of a provision of the New York Code of Rules and Regulations permitting the state to offset special advance payments for rent from subsequent AFDC grants. The welfare recipients claimed that the offset regulation violated the equal protection clause and pertinent federal statutes governing the AFDC program and federal regulations issued pursuant thereto. Federal jurisdiction was invoked under 28 U.S. Code, 1343(3), which confers original jurisdiction upon federal district courts to adjudicate claims based upon a denial of constitutional rights under color of state law. The district court concluded that jurisdiction over the equal protection claim existed under section 1343(3), thereby providing a basis for pendent jurisdiction to adjudicate the corollary "statutory" claim. The district court then held that the challenged offset regulation was invalid under the Social Security Act and certain federal regulations. The court of appeals reversed, holding that the equal protection claim was so insubstantial that the district court lacked jurisdiction over either that claim or the statutory claim.

Question: Did the district court have jurisdiction to adjudicate both the equal protection and statutory claims?

Decision: Yes. Opinion by Justice White. Vote: 6–3, Powell, Rehnquist, and Burger dissenting.

Reasons: On its face, the welfare recipients' equal protection claim challenging a New York state regulation fell within the jurisdictional standards of section 1343(3), because it alleged that constitutional rights were being denied under color of state law. However, prior Supreme Court decisions have held that clearly insubstantial constitutional claims do not confer jurisdiction under section 1343(3). The court of appeals reasoned that the state offset regulation was obviously constitutional because it had the rational objective of providing an incentive for welfare recipients to properly manage their grants and prevented those who did not from being preferred over those who did. However, even accepting the reasoning of the court of appeals, the equal protection claim had sufficient merit to confer jurisdiction under section 1343(3).

The district court jurisdiction over the constitutional claim provided a basis for adjudicating the statutory claim under the doctrine of pendent jurisdiction. That doctrine, as enunciated in *United Mine Workers* v. *Gibbs*, 383 U.S. 715 (1966), authorizes a federal court to adjudicate a claim over which it has no independent jurisdiction if the claim grows out of the same set of operative facts that generated the claim conferring jurisdiction. In this case, the statutory and equal protection claims rested on the same set of facts. Although *Gibbs* held that a federal district court has the authority to abstain from deciding pendent claims, the Court concluded that this authority should rarely be exercised when the pendent claim rests upon federal rather than state law.

Pernell v. Southall Realty, 416 U.S. 363 (1974)

Facts: A tenant requested a jury trial in an eviction action brought by his landlord. The landlord sued under a District of Columbia statute that provided a remedy for "any person" aggrieved by a wrongful detention of real property. Rejecting the claim that the Seventh Amendment guaranteed the tenant a right to a jury trial, the trial judge heard the case himself and entered judgment for the landlord.

Question: Was the tenant entitled to a jury trial under the Seventh Amendment?

Decision: Yes. Opinion by Justice Marshall. Vote: 9–0.

Reasons: The Seventh Amendment guarantees a litigant in federal court a right to a jury trial "[i]n suits at common law, where the value in controversy shall exceed twenty dollars. . . ." That amendment, "[l]ike other provisions in the Bill of Rights, . . . is fully applicable to courts established by Congress in the District of Columbia." Under the Seventh Amendment, a litigant is guaranteed a jury trial (1) if the common law as it existed in 1791 would have required a jury trial, or (2) if the lawsuit "involves rights and remedies of the sort traditionally enforced in an action at law, rather than in an action at equity or admiralty." In this case, the tenant had a Seventh Amendment right to a jury trial under either test. If his landlord had sought to evict him in 1791 under the various forms of action that the common law developed for the recovery of the possession of real property rather than in 1971, the tenant would clearly have had a right to jury trial. Additionally, the right to recover possession of real property was a right protected at common law and not in equity or admiralty.

The Court indicated, however, "that the Seventh Amendment would not be a bar to a congressional effort to entrust landlord-tenant disputes, including those over the right to possession, to an administrative agency." The Court interpreted its earlier decision in *Block* v. *Hirsh*, 256 U.S. 135 (1921), to stand "for the principle that the Seventh Amendment is generally inapplicable in administrative proceedings where jury trials would be incompatible with the whole concept of administrative adjudication."

Curtis v. *Loether*, 415 U.S. 189 (1974)

Facts: A Negro woman brought suit under section 812 of the Civil Rights Act of 1968 alleging that she had been illegally refused housing on account of her race. Seeking actual and punitive damages, the woman demanded a jury trial. That demand was opposed on the grounds that neither section 812 nor the Seventh Amendment entitled the woman to a jury trial.

Question: Does the Seventh Amendment give the woman a right to trial by jury on her claim brought under section 812 in federal court?

Decision: Yes. Opinion by Justice Marshall. Vote: 9–0.

Reasons: Whether section 812 was intended to afford a right to jury trial is uncertain and unnecessary to decide, because "it is clear that the Seventh Amendment entitles either party to demand a jury trial in an action for damages in the federal courts under section 812." The Seventh Amendment preserves the right to jury trial in actions seeking to enforce legal rights and remedies, whether created by statute or by common law, as opposed to suits in equity or admiralty jurisdiction. A damage action under section 812 is an action to enforce "legal rights" within the meaning of the Seventh Amendment for two reasons: (1) the relief sought (actual and punitive damages) is the traditional form of relief offered in the courts of law as opposed to courts of equity; and (2) a claim under section 812 is analogous to a tort action brought under common law. That section authorizes the courts to compensate a plaintiff for the injury caused by a defendant's wrongful breach of a legal duty created by statute.

The Court left open the question of whether the Seventh Amendment guaranteed a right of jury trial in every suit seeking monetary relief, such as suits seeking reinstatement and back pay for wrongful discharge.

O'Shea v. Littleton, 414 U.S. 488 (1974)

Facts: Nineteen individuals in Cairo, Illinois, brought a federal civil rights action against several persons connected with the administration of criminal justice, including two state judges. Requesting injunctive relief, the complaint alleged that the state judges had violated the constitutional rights of the plaintiffs in connection with the setting of bail, the imposition of sentences, and the assessment of costs for jury trial in criminal cases. Each of these continuing practices was alleged to have been carried out intentionally to deprive the plaintiffs of the protections of the county criminal justice system and to deter them from engaging in an economic boycott and similar activities. The district court dismissed the case on the grounds that it lacked jurisdiction to issue the requested injunctive relief and that the judges were immune from suit for acts done in connection with their official duties. On review in the Supreme Court, the issue of whether the complaint alleged a sufficiently concrete controversy to fall within the Article III jurisdiction of the federal courts was raised.

Questions: (1) Did the complaint satisfy the threshold requirement imposed by Article III of the Constitution that those who seek to invoke the power of federal courts must allege an actual case or controversy? (2) Did the complaint state a valid basis for injunctive relief against the state judges?

Decision: No to both questions. Opinion by Justice White. Vote: 6–3 on the first question and 5–4 on the second. Blackmun concurred on question (1) and dissented on question (2); Douglas, Brennan, and Marshall dissented on both.

Reasons: Article III, section 2 of the Constitution limits the federal judicial power to "Cases" and "Controversies." That limitation requires that plaintiffs in the federal courts allege a "real and immediate" injury or threat of injury as contrasted with "conjectural" or "hypothetical" injuries. In this case, the complaint failed to allege that any of the plaintiffs had suffered actual injury at the hands of the defendant judges, or contemplated threatened injury because of an imminent criminal prosecution. The plaintiffs alleged in substance only that if they violate a valid law and if they are charged, held to answer, and tried in any proceedings before the defendants, then they will be subject to the unconstitutional practices the defendants allegedly follow. That alleged injury is too conjectural and speculative to qualify as a case or controversy within the meaning of Article III.

Even if the complaint alleged an existing case or controversy, it did not allege an adequate basis for equitable relief. It is well established that the "concurrent operation of federal and state courts counsels restraint against the issuance of injunctions against state officers engaged in the administration of the State's criminal laws. . . ." The purpose of that rule is to prevent "unwarranted anticipatory interference in the state criminal process by means of continuous or piecemeal interruptions of the State proceedings by litigation in the federal courts. . . ." The plaintiffs' requested injunctive relief contemplated the continuous supervision by the federal court over the conduct of the defendant judges in criminal cases, immediate interruption of those state proceedings if noncompliance with the injunction were alleged, and a contempt order against the defendants if noncompliance were proven. Such federal intrusion into the daily conduct of state criminal proceedings is inconsistent with the principles of comity between state and federal courts which prior case law has established.

Additionally, the complaint failed to allege immediate, irreparable injury and inadequate remedies at law. Proof of such allegations is necessary to establish a right to injunctive relief. The complaint, however, alleged only speculative injury; and the alleged unconstitutional misconduct of the judges could be adequately remedied through change of venue, their disqualification, direct appeal, habeas corpus, and the threat of federal criminal prosecution.

Scherk v. Alberto-Culver Co., 417 U.S. 506 (1974)

Facts: Alberto-Culver Co., an American manufacturer with its principal office in Illinois, brought suit in federal district court against a German citizen (Scherk) alleging a violation of section 10(b) of the Securities Exchange Act of 1934 and rule 10b-5 promulgated thereunder. The complaint alleged that Scherk made fraudulent and misleading representations in connection with the sale of three of his companies to Alberto-Culver. Scherk moved to dismiss the complaint on the ground, *inter alia,* that the contract of sale provided for arbitration of "any controversy or claim" arising out of the agreement before the International Chamber of Commerce in Paris, France. The district court denied the motion, reasoning that an agreement to arbitrate could not preclude a purchaser from suing under rule 10b-5 in light of section 29(a) of the act. That section provides in part that "[a]ny . . . stipulation, or provision binding any person to waive compliance with any . . . rule [promulgated under the act] shall be void."

Question: Did the arbitration clause in the sales agreement bar Alberto-Culver's rule 10b-5 suit?

Decision: Yes. Opinion by Justice Stewart. Vote: 5–4, Douglas, Brennan, White, and Marshall dissenting.

Reasons: Section 4 of the Arbitration Act of 1925 "directs a federal court to order parties to proceed to arbitration if there has been a 'failure, neglect, or refusal' of any party to honor an agreement to arbitrate." This strong policy in favor of arbitration should not be rejected under the circumstances of this case, notwithstanding the policy against waiver of rights under the act embodied in section 29(a).

It is argued that *Wilko v. Swan*, 346 U.S. 427 (1953), compels a contrary result. There a purchaser of stock sued a brokerage firm alleging a violation of the Securities Act of 1933, despite an agreement with the firm to arbitrate the dispute. The Court held that the agreement to arbitrate was null and void under a nonwaiver provision of the Securities Act comparable to section 29(a). In contrast, the arbitration clause questioned here was part of a "truly international agreement."

> A contractual provision specifying in advance the forum in which disputes shall be litigated and the law to be applied is . . . an almost indispensable precondition to achievement of the orderliness and predictability essential to any international business transaction. . . . [S]uch a provision obviates the danger that a dispute under the agreement might be submitted to a forum hostile to the interests of one of the parties or unfamiliar with the problem area involved.

These international implications of the arbitration clause in this case clearly distinguish it from the arbitration agreement in *Wilko:*

> We cannot have trade and commerce in world markets and international waters exclusively on our terms, governed by our laws, and resolved in our courts. . . . [Accordingly] the agreement of the parties in this case to arbitrate any dispute arising out of their international commercial transaction is to be respected and enforced by the federal courts in accord with the explicit provisions of the Arbitration Act.

Sex Discrimination

The women's rights movement has lead to a heightened awareness of sex discrimination and to a proposed equal rights amendment to the Constitution. Increased sensitivity concerning sex discrimination has undoubtedly been partially responsible for litigation that has resulted in several recent Supreme Court decisions on the subject. In *Reed* v. *Reed*, 404 U.S. 71 (1971), the Court held unconstitutional a provision in the Idaho probate code that gave preference to men in the appointment of administrators of estates. The Court concluded that the equal protection clause requires that discrimination based upon sex have a "fair and substantial relation" to the object of the legislation. In *Frontiero* v. *Richardson*, 411 U.S. 677 (1973), the Court declared unconstitutional certain provisions of the U.S. Code which made it easier for servicemen than for servicewomen to claim their spouses as dependents for purposes of receiving certain government benefits. Four of the justices in *Frontiero* thought that sex discrimination, like racial discrimination, should be viewed by the courts as inherently suspect and thus subject to close judicial scrutiny.

During this term, the Court decided four cases concerning sex discrimination. Although three of the decisions tended to favor elimination of sexual bias, the justices failed to agree that sex discrimination could be justified only by a compelling state interest.

In a case concerning mandatory maternity leave for public school teachers, the Court held unconstitutional certain rules that required teachers to terminate their employment several months before expected childbirth and prohibited re-employment for several months thereafter. The Court concluded that the employment status of pregnant teachers before and after childbirth should be considered on an individual basis in light of the physical abilities of the particular teacher involved. In another employment case, the Court held that a company had violated the Equal Pay Act of 1963 by paying higher wages to male night inspectors than to female day inspectors.

In a third case concerning alleged discrimination against men, the Court upheld the constitutionality of a Florida statute granting property tax exemptions to widows but not to widowers. The Court reasoned that the historic economic discrimination against women justified remedial legislation which gave women preferred status. Passage of the equal rights amendment, however, could in effect reverse this decision.

In a case concerning a state disability insurance system which excluded disabilities related to pregnancy, the Court ruled that the exclusion was not based upon distinctions of sex and hence was constitutionally sound.

Although the Court's decisions in recent years have expanded women's rights, many leaders of the women's rights movement probably will remain unsatisfied with their legal status until the equal rights amendment is adopted. Approved by Congress and as of this writing ratified by thirty-four of the thirty-eight states needed for adoption, the amendment would provide that "[e]quality of rights under the law shall not be denied or abridged by the United States or by any State on account of sex." If it is adopted, the amendment will undoubtedly spawn litigation that would threaten present laws that give special protection and preferences to women.

Cleveland Board of Education v. *La Fleur*, 414 U.S. 632 (1974)

Facts: Several public school teachers brought suit challenging the constitutionality of mandatory maternity leave rules of the Cleveland, Ohio, and Chesterfield County, Virginia, school boards. Under the Cleveland rule, pregnant teachers must take unpaid maternity leave five months before the expected childbirth and apply for such leave at least two weeks before departure. In addition, eligibility to return to work is not accorded until the commencement of the next regular semester after the child is three months old and is contingent upon medical certification of the teacher's health. The Chesterfield County rule requires teachers to leave work at least four months, and to give notice at least six months, prior to anticipated childbirth. Re-employment is guaranteed a teacher on maternity leave no later than the first day of the school year following the date when she is physically fit and able to assure that her child will not interfere with her job. The pregnant teachers contended that the Cleveland and Chesterfield County mandatory maternity leave rules were unconstitutionally arbitrary in violation of the Fourteenth Amendment.

Question: Do the challenged mandatory leave rules create an irrebuttable presumption that pregnant teachers will be physically incapable of performing their duties during the latter part of pregnancy and during three months thereafter in violation of due process?

Decision: Yes. Opinion by Justice Stewart. Vote: 7–2, Rehnquist and Burger dissenting.

Reasons: Because public school maternity leave rules directly affect the fundamental civil right to "decide to bear children," "the Due Process Clause of the Fourteenth Amendment requires that such rules must not needlessly, arbitrarily, or capriciously impinge upon this vital area of a teacher's constitutional liberty." The school boards contend that their mandatory maternity leave rules are necessary to maintain continuity in classroom instruction and to assure the presence of a physically capable instructor in the classroom at all times.

Continuity, however, is accomplished by requiring ample notice of departure. In fact, since the fourth or fifth month of each pregnancy will occur at different times during the school year, the challenged rules often compel departure during mid-semester thereby hindering "attainment of the very continuity objectives that they are purportedly designed to promote." The goal of making certain that an instructor is physically capable was accomplished in this case by an irrebuttable presumption of physical incompetency in the later months of pregnancy, in spite of the fact that "the medical evidence as to an individual woman's physical status might be wholly to the contrary." The medical experts in these cases agreed that the ability of any particular pregnant woman to continue at work past any fixed time in her pregnancy is very much an individual matter. Thus, the conclusive presumption of physical disability embodied in the challenged rules is neither "necessarily nor universally true" and violates the due process clause. The Court, however, left open the question of whether a mandatory leave date during the last weeks of pregnancy might be justified.

Regarding limitations placed upon a teacher's eligibility to return to work after giving birth, the Court upheld the rules insofar as they required a medical certification of physical health and delay until the commencement of the next semester or school year following delivery. The Court concluded that those limitations were necessary to assure continuity in teaching and the physical capability of the instructor. However, the Court held that the additional Cleveland limitation absolutely forbidding a teacher from returning to work until her child reaches the age of three months was unreasonable and suffered from "the same constitutional deficiencies that plague the irrebuttable presumption in the termination rules."

Corning Glass Works v. Brennan, 417 U.S. 188 (1974)

Facts: Between 1925 and 1930, Corning Glass Works hired only males to perform night-shift inspection, and these men received wages higher than those paid to women performing day-shift inspection. In 1944, a collective-bargaining agreement provided for a plantwide wage differential for day and night work that was superimposed on the existing base wage difference between male night inspectors and female day inspectors. Beginning in 1966, Corning began to open up jobs on the night shift to women. On 20 January 1969, Corning began to pay all subsequently hired inspectors the same wage whatever their sex or shift. However, employees hired before that date continued to receive a higher wage rate for working the night shift, thereby perpetuating the differential in base pay between day and night inspectors. The secretary of labor brought suit seeking to enjoin Corning from violating the Equal Pay Act of 1963 and to collect back wages allegedly due female employees because of past violations. That act requires employers to offer equal pay regardless of sex for "work performed under similar working conditions," though it allows certain exceptions.

Corning argued that day-shift work was not "performed under similar working conditions" as those of night-shift work. Thus, different wage rates for male night-shift inspectors and female day-shift inspectors did not violate the act.

Questions: (1) Did Corning violate the Equal Pay Act when it paid male night-shift inspectors more than it did female day-shift inspectors? (2) If so, did Corning comply fully with the act when in 1966 it began to hire women to work as night-shift inspectors? (3) If the violation was not remedied in 1966, did Corning come into compliance with the law in 1969 by equalizing day and night inspector wage rates while maintaining higher rates for employees hired prior to 1969 and working the night shift?

Decision: Yes to question (1) and no to questions (2) and (3). Opinion by Justice Marshall. Vote: 5–3, Burger, Blackmun, and Rehnquist dissenting. Stewart did not participate.

Reasons: The legislative history of the Equal Pay Act clearly shows that the phrase "working conditions" includes physical surroundings and hazards and excludes the time of day worked. Accordingly, the payment of wages that were higher for male night inspectors than for female day inspectors violated the act. Corning did not remedy this violation in 1966 by opening up night-shift jobs to females. The act required that Corning raise the depressed wages of the female day-shift inspectors to the level of those earned by the male night-shift inspectors. Similarly, the action Corning took in 1969 perpetuated the effects of its prior illegal practice of paying women less than men for equal work.

> While the [1969 plan] provided for equal base wages for night or day inspectors hired after that date, it continued to provide unequal base wages for employees hired before that date. . . . [I]t is clear from the record that had the company equalized the base wage rates of male and female inspectors on the effective date of the Act, as the law required, the day inspectors in 1969 would have been entitled to the same higher . . . rate the company provided for night inspectors.

Accordingly, the Court held that the secretary of labor was entitled to the requested relief.

Kahn v. Shevin, 416 U.S. 351 (1974)

Facts: A Florida statute granting to widows but not to widowers an annual $500 property tax exemption was challenged as a violation of equal protection because invidiously discriminating against males.

Question: Does the Florida statute violate the equal protection clause of the Fourteenth Amendment?

Decision: No. Opinion by Justice Douglas. Vote 6–3, Brennan, Marshall, and White dissenting.

Reasons: Whether because of overt discrimination or cultural reasons, a woman's income is on the average far less than a man's. "The disparity is likely to be exacerbated for the widow. While the widower can usually continue in the occupation which preceded his spouse's death, in many cases the widow will find herself suddenly forced into a job market with which she is unfamiliar, and in which, because of her former economic dependency, she will have fewer skills to offer." The purpose of the challenged statute is to reduce the economic disparity between widows and widowers. The statute's discriminatory treatment meets constitutional standards under *Reed* v. *Reed*, 404 U.S. 71 (1971), because it "rest[s] upon some ground of difference having a fair and substantial relation to the object of the legislation." Rejecting the contention that the sex discrimination could only be upheld if justified by a compelling state interest, the Court concluded that states have large leeway in making classifications for tax purposes.

Geduldig v. Aiello, 417 U.S. 484 (1974)

Facts: California's disability insurance system covers private employees who are temporarily disabled from working by a disability not covered by workmen's compensation. The insurance system is funded entirely from contributions deducted from the wages of employees, who are legally required to contribute unless protected by an alternate system approved by the state. Generally speaking, the insurance protects against any disability caused by mental or physical illness or injury, but it excludes a disability accompanying normal pregnancy. The disability insurance system was challenged as violative of the equal protection clause on the theory that it invidiously discriminates against women by failing to pay insurance benefits for disability that accompanies normal pregnancy and childbirth.

Question: Does the challenged California disability insurance system discriminate against women in violation of equal protection?

Decision: No. Opinion by Justice Stewart. Vote: 6–3, Brennan, Douglas, and Marshall dissenting.

Reasons: "Although California has created a program to insure most risks of employment disability, it has not chosen to insure all such risks, and this decision is reflected in the level of annual contribution exacted from participating employees." With respect to social welfare programs like this one, classifications with a rational basis are constitutional. The state's purpose in excluding disabilities accompanying normal pregnancies from insurance coverage was to maintain the contribution rate at a low level by reducing benefit payments. That purpose provides "an objective and wholly non-invidious basis for the State's decision not to create a more comprehensive insurance program than it has."

The Court declined to characterize the alleged discrimination as one based upon sex. The Court reasoned that under the insurance program, "[t]here is no risk from which men are protected and women are not. Likewise, there is no risk from which women are protected and men are not."

Government Benefits

The combined budgets of federal, state and local governments now exceed $400 billion. Approximately seventeen million employees now work for the government at some level. The fact that government benefits and government employment is important to a growing number of persons has caused increased litigation over these matters. This term the Court decided cases concerning welfare benefits, veterans' benefits, social security, and government employment preference for Indians.

Following a series of decisions beginning in 1968 affording scrupulous constitutional protection to the rights of illegitimate children, the Court held unconstitutional a provision of the Social Security Act that denied illegitimate children certain disability benefits.

In a 5–4 decision that could have a sweeping impact on the administration of welfare programs, the Court held that the Eleventh Amendment prohibited the recovery of welfare benefits that had been illegally withheld by a state government. Considering the growing fiscal burden that welfare benefits place on state budgets, this

113

decision may encourage states to violate the requirements of certain welfare laws. In another welfare case, the Court struck down a one-year residency requirement for free nonemergency medical care.

With regard to veterans' educational benefits, the Court held that such benefits could constitutionally be denied to conscientious objectors who performed alternate civilian service. The Court also upheld the validity of federal law granting Indians employment preference in the Bureau of Indian Affairs. Because the purpose of the preference was to encourage Indian self-government, a nonracially based goal, the case did not raise the issue of whether affirmative action programs intended to benefit particular races are constitutional.

Jimenez v. Weinberger, 417 U.S. 628 (1974)

Facts: Under the Social Security Act, illegitimate children are eligible to receive disability insurance benefits if (1) state law permits them to inherit from the disabled parent, (2) their illegitimacy results solely from technical defects in their parents' ceremonial marriage, or (3) they are legitimated in accordance with state law. An illegitimate child unable to qualify for benefits under the foregoing conditions can qualify only if the disabled parent contributed to the child's support or lived with him prior to the disability. Denied disability benefits because they were born after the onset of their parents' disability, illegitimate children brought suit claiming that the Social Security Act's arbitrary treatment of different classes of illegitimate children violated due process.

Question: For purposes of determining eligibility for disability insurance benefits, is the Social Security Act's classification of illegitimate children so arbitrary as to violate due process?

Decision: Yes. Opinion by Chief Justice Burger. Vote: 8–1, Rehnquist dissenting.

Reasons: Under the act, illegitimate children born after the onset of a parent's disability are divided into two classes. "[The first class of] children [is] deemed entitled to receive benefits without showing that they are in fact dependent upon their disabled parent. The second [class] of after-born illegitimate children includes those who are conclusively denied benefits because they do not fall within one of the foregoing categories and are not entitled to receive insurance benefits under any other provision of the Act." The asserted purpose for excluding the second class of illegitimate children from benefits is to prevent spurious claims. However, the record in this case shows that "the potential for spurious claims is the same as to both [classes]; hence to conclusively deny one [class] benefits presumptively available to the other denies the former the equal protection of the law guaranteed by the due process provisions of the Fifth Amendment."

Edelman v. Jordan, 415 U.S. 651 (1974)

Facts: Under the jointly funded federal-state programs of Aid to the Aged, Blind and Disabled (AABD), participating states, as a condition to receiving federal funds, must process and make grants to eligible recipients within certain time limits. Illinois AABD recipients successfully contended in federal district court that Illinois officials were violating the federally imposed time limits for processing and making grants in the administration of the AABD program. The district court enjoined the state officials from violating the federal time limits and ordered the payment of retroactive benefits to AABD recipients whose benefits had been illegally withheld. The Illinois officials contended that the award of retroactive benefits was prohibited by the Eleventh Amendment which generally bars federal court jurisdiction over citizen suits against a state.

Question: Does the Eleventh Amendment bar the award against a state of retroactive benefits to AABD recipients who have been illegally denied those benefits?

Decision: Yes. Opinion by Justice Rehnquist. Vote: 5–4, Douglas, Brennan, Marshall, and Blackmun dissenting.

Reasons: The Eleventh Amendment provides that federal courts may not entertain "any suit in law or equity, commenced or prosecuted against one of the United States by Citizens of another State. . . ." The Court has consistently interpreted the amendment to bar suit against an unconsenting state in federal court brought by her own citizens as well as by citizens of another state. Prior Supreme Court decisions have also established the rule "that a suit by private parties seeking to impose a liability which must be paid from public funds in the state treasury is barred by the Eleventh Amendment." The challenged award of retroactive AABD benefits in this case "will to a virtual certainty be paid from state funds . . ." and thus violates the Eleventh Amendment.

The Court also rejected the contention that Illinois had waived its Eleventh Amendment protection by participating in the federally established AABD programs. Noting that Congress had not unambiguously required states to waive their immunity from suit as a prerequisite for participation in the programs, the Court concluded that such a waiver could not properly be inferred. The Court reasoned that "[i]n deciding whether a State has waived its constitutional protection under the Eleventh Amendment, we will find waiver only where stated 'by the most express language or by such overwhelming implications from the text as will leave no room for any other reasonable construction.' "

Memorial Hospital v. Maricopa County, 415 U.S. 250 (1974)

Facts: Henry Evaro, an indigent suffering from a chronic asthmatic and bronchial illness, challenged the constitutionality of an Arizona statute requiring a year's residence in a county as a condition to receiving nonemergency hospitalization or medical care at the county's expense. Evaro contended that the one-year residency provision violated the equal protection clause by discriminating against otherwise eligible individuals who had recently exercised their constitutional right of interstate travel.

Question: Does Arizona's county residency requirement imposed as a condition to receiving free nonemergency medical care, as applied to residents who have moved from another state, violate the equal protection clause?

Decision: Yes. Opinion by Justice Marshall. Vote: 8–1, Douglas filed a separate opinion and Rehnquist dissented.

Reasons: Shapiro v. Thompson, 394 U.S. 618 (1969), established the proposition that a state law restricting the right of interstate travel could be upheld under the equal protection clause only if that penalty could be justified by a compelling state interest. The challenged Arizona provision penalizes indigent new residents who have recently traveled interstate by excluding them from the receipt of "a basic necessity of life"—free nonemergency medical care—for one year. Thus, only a compelling state interest can constitutionally justify the one-year exclusion.

Arizona contends that a one-year waiting period is necessary to ensure the fiscal integrity of its free medical care program by discouraging an influx of indigents, to prevent fraudulent claims by nonresidents, and to predict budgetary needs. None of those three justifications serves a compelling state interest. "First, a State may not protect the public fisc by drawing an invidious distinction between classes of its citizens. . . ." Second, the durational residency requirement is not necessary to prevent fraud because state law makes it a crime to file an "untrue statement" for the purpose of obtaining free medical care. Third, Arizona has failed to show that it in fact uses the one-year residency requirement to predict the number of people who will require assistance in the budget year.

Johnson v. Robison, 415 U.S. 361 (1974)

Facts: A three-judge federal district court held unconstitutional certain provisions of the Veterans Readjustment Act of 1966 which denied veterans' educational benefits to conscientious objectors who performed alternate civilian service. The district court concluded that such denial invidiously discriminated against conscientious objectors in violation of due process. The Veterans Administration contended that (1) federal courts are barred under 38 U.S. Code, 211(a) from deciding the constitutionality of veterans' benefits legislation, and (2) Congress had a rational and constitutional basis for conferring educational benefits upon veterans but not upon conscientious objectors.

Questions: (1) Are federal courts barred by statute from determining the constitutionality of veterans' benefits legislation? (2) Do provisions of the Veterans Readjustment Act which deny educational benefits to conscientious objectors violate due process?

Decision: No to both questions. Opinion by Justice Brennan. Vote: 8–1, Douglas dissenting.

Reasons: 38 U.S. Code, 211(a) bars judicial review "only of those decisions of law or fact that arise in the *administration* by the Veterans' Administration of a *statute* providing benefits for veterans." The constitutional challenge in this case "is not to any such decision of the *Administrator*, but rather to a decision of *Congress* to create a statutory class entitled to benefits that does not include . . . conscientious objectors who performed alternate civilian service." Thus, the constitutional question raised is not immune from judicial review under section 211(a). A statute will not be construed to restrict access to judicial review unless Congress provides clear and convincing evidence that such a result was intended.

Turning to the merits, the objectives of Congress in enacting the act were to: (1) make service in the Armed Forces more attractive; (2) extend the benefits of higher education to those who might not otherwise be able to afford such an education; (3) provide vocational readjustment and restore lost educational opportunities to those whose careers had been interrupted by reason of active duty; and (4) aid persons in attaining the vocational and educational status which they might have attained had they not served their country. In light of these objectives, Congress could rationally exclude conscientious objectors from the act's benefits, because the disruption caused by military service is both quantitatively and qualitatively different from that caused by alternate civilian service. Moreover, that exclusion also bears a rational relation to making service in the Armed Forces more attractive to those who are willing to serve. "[B]ecause a conscientious objector bases his refusal to serve in the Armed Forces upon deeply held religious beliefs, we will not assume that educational benefits will make military service more attractive to him."

The Court also rejected the claim that the act's denial of benefits to alternate service conscientious objectors interfered with their free exercise of religion under the First Amendment by penalizing adherence to their religious beliefs. The Court reasoned that the government's substantial interest in raising and supporting armies, furthered by an act advancing the "neutral, secular governmental interests of enhancing military service and aiding the readjustment of military personnel from military to civilian life," justified the alleged burden on the free exercise of religion.

Morton v. Mancari, 417 U.S. 535 (1974)

Facts: The Indian Reorganization Act of 1934 accords an employment preference for qualified Indians in the Bureau of Indian Affairs (BIA). That preference was challenged in federal district court as contrary to (1) the Equal Employment Opportunity Act of 1972 which forbids racial discrimination in most federal employment, and (2) the due process clause of the Fifth Amendment. The district court concluded that preference given to Indians under the 1934 act was impliedly repealed by the 1972 act.

Questions: (1) Was the Indian preference in the 1934 act impliedly repealed by the 1972 act? (2) If not, does the Indian preference violate due process?

Decision: No to both questions. Opinion by Justice Blackmun. Vote: 9–0.

Reasons: The overriding purpose of the 1934 act "was to establish machinery whereby Indian tribes would be able to assume a greater degree of self-government, both politically and economically. . . . One of the primary means by which self-government would be fostered and the Bureau [of Indian Affairs] made more responsive was to increase the participation of tribal Indians in the BIA operations. In order to achieve this end, it was recognized that some kind of preference and exemption from otherwise prevailing civil service requirements was necessary."

It is contended that the 1972 act proscribing racial discrimination in government repealed by implication the provision in the 1934 act that calls for employment preference for Indians in the Bureau of Indian Affairs. However, repeals by implication are not favored by the courts. The legislative history of the 1972 act does not reflect an intent to nullify the Indian preference in the 1934 act. "[W]hen two statutes are capable of co-existence, it is the duty of the courts, absent a clearly expressed congressional intention to the contrary, to regard each as effective." Accordingly, the district court erred in ruling that the Indian preference was repealed by the 1972 act.

It is next contended that the preference constitutes invidious racial discrimination in violation of due process. Congress has plenary power to deal with the special problems of Indians under Article I, section 8, clause 3. That clause provides Congress with the power to "regulate Commerce . . . with the Indian Tribes." The special treatment accorded Indians under the 1934 act is not really a "racial" preference but is "an employment criterion reasonably designed to further the cause of Indian self-government and to make the BIA more responsive to the needs of its constituent groups." Because the "preference is reasonably and directly related to a legitimate, non-racially based goal," it does not violate due process.

Labor Law

At least in part reflecting the importance of employment to individuals and the strength of labor unions, the Supreme Court has in recent years decided several labor law cases each term. The Court's decisions cannot fairly be characterized as either pro- or anti-labor. Generally speaking, the Court has ordered the arbitration of labor disputes whenever a permissible interpretation of an applicable statute would permit such an order. However, the Court departed from its general doctrine of favoring arbitration this term in holding that a purchaser of a company had no obligation to arbitrate with the union having a collective-bargaining agreement with the seller. In another case, however, the Court relied on a strong policy favoring arbitration in ordering arbitration of a safety dispute.

The Court made certain decisions that might be characterized as being unfavorable to unions:

—No "managerial" employees are entitled to organize under the National Labor Relations Act.

—State laws permitting supervisors who are discharged because of union membership to sue for damages are prohibited by the National Labor Relations Act.

—A union in seeking recognition may not offer to waive initiation fees for only those employees who sign "recognition slips."

—State courts may enjoin a strike in violation of a collective bargaining agreement although the strike arguably constitutes an unfair labor practice under the National Labor Relations Act.

—In determining whether a real estate management company does sufficient business to fall within the minimum wage and overtime provisions of the Fair Labor Standards Act, the amount of its gross commissions rather than gross rentals collected should be used.

The Court made the following decisions that might be characterized as favorable to unions:

—The purchaser of a business that has committed an unfair labor practice by discharging an employee may be ordered to reinstate that employee with back pay.

—A union may discipline a supervisory employee who is a union member for performing rank-and-file work during a strike.

—A company may not absolutely prohibit the distribution of union literature on its premises even though a collective-bargaining agreement authorizes such a ban.

—A union organizing federal employees may not be sued for libel during an organization drive without proof that a defamatory statement was made with actual malice.

—Federal law does not prohibit employment discrimination based upon lack of citizenship.

Howard Johnson Co., Inc. v. Detroit Local Joint Executive Board, Hotel and Restaurant Employees, 417 U.S. 249 (1974)

Facts: Howard Johnson Company purchased the personal property used in connection with a restaurant and motor lodge business under an agreement whereby the seller retained ownership of the real property and leased it to the company. The agreement also provided that the company would not recognize and assume any obligations arising from a collective-bargaining agreement between the seller and a union. The company proceeded to hire forty-five employees to operate the restaurant and motor lodge, nine of whom were the seller's former employees. Characterizing the failure of Howard Johnson to hire all of the seller's employees as a "lockout" in violation of its collective-bargaining agreements with the seller, the union brought suit seeking an order compelling Howard Johnson to arbitrate the extent of its obligations to the union under the seller's agreements. A federal district court concluded that under *John Wiley and Sons* v. *Livingston*, 376 U.S. 543 (1964), the company was a "successor" to the seller and thus ordered the requested arbitration.

Question: Was the Howard Johnson Company required to arbitrate the extent of its obligations to the union under the so-called "successorship" doctrine announced in *Wiley*?

Decision: No. Opinion by Justice Marshall. Vote 8–1, Douglas dissenting.

Reasons: "In *Wiley*, the Union representing the employees of a corporation which had disappeared through a merger sought to compel the surviving corporation, which had hired all of the merged corporation's employees and continued to operate the enterprise in a substantially identical form after the merger, to arbitrate under the merged corporation's collective-bargaining agreement." The Court held that

> the disappearance by merger of a corporate employer which has entered into a collective bargaining agreement with a union does not automatically terminate all rights of the employees covered by the agreement, and that, in appropriate circumstances, present here, the successor employer may be required to arbitrate with the union under the agreement.

This case, however, is clearly distinguishable from *Wiley*. There, requiring arbitration may have been "fairly within the reasonable expectations of the parties because applicable state law made the surviving corporation in a merger liable for the obligations of the disappearing corporation." Here, the company expressly disclaimed the assumption of any obligations under the seller's collective-bargaining agreement. There, the disappearance of the original corporate party to the collective-bargaining agreement meant that unless the union were afforded a remedy against the surviving corporation its collective-bargaining rights would vanish. Here, the seller agreed to arbitrate the extent of its liability to the union under the collective-bargaining agreement. There, the surviving corporation hired all of the employees of the disappearing corporation. Here, only nine of the fifty-three seller's employees were hired by the company.

Additionally, *Wiley* held that arbitration could not be required of a "successor employer" unless there was a "substantial continuity of identity in the business enterprise" before and after a change of ownership. "This continuity of identity in the business enterprise necessarily includes . . . a substantial continuity in the identity of the work force across the change in ownership. . . . Since there was plainly no substantial continuity of identity in the work force hired by [the purchaser] with that of the [seller], and no express or implied assumption of the agreement to arbitrate . . . compelling the Company to arbitrate the extent of its obligations to the former [seller's] employees" was erroneous.

Gateway Coal Co. v. United Mine Workers of America, 414 U.S. 368 (1974)

Facts: Certain foremen at a Gateway Coal Company mine were suspended for falsifying records to show no air flow reduction at the mine when in fact the air flow had been substantially reduced because of the collapse of a ventilation structure. When the company reinstated the foremen while criminal charges were pending against them, the miners, represented by the United Mine Workers (UMW), struck to protest the alleged safety hazard created by the presence of the foremen in the mines. After the union refused to arbitrate the dispute, Gateway sued under section 301 of the Labor Management Relations Act seeking to compel arbitration and to enjoin the strike. Concluding that a broad arbitration clause in the collective-bargaining agreement between Gateway and the union governed the dispute, the district court granted Gateway the requested relief. The court of appeals reversed on the ground that public policy disfavored compulsory arbitration of safety disputes and that without an express provision for arbitration the United Mine Workers had no duty to arbitrate and hence no implied obligation not to strike.

Question: Did the Gateway-UMW agreement impose on the parties a duty to arbitrate safety disputes, and did this agreement imply a no-strike obligation that could be enforced by an injunction?

Decision: Yes. Opinion by Justice Powell. Vote: 8–1, Douglas dissenting.

Reasons: The agreement provides for arbitration over disputes concerning its meaning and application, disputes about matters not specifically mentioned in the agreement, and disputes concerning local trouble of any kind. The instant safety dispute concerning the presence of foremen at a local mine concerns "local trouble" subject to arbitration under the agreement. The court of appeals erroneously concluded that public policy should not favor arbitration of safety disputes contrary to the well-established Supreme Court rule that arbitration of grievances should not be denied "unless it may be said with positive assurance that the arbitration clause is not susceptible of an interpretation that covers the asserted dispute." The purpose of that rule, to prevent industrial strife and to encourage settlements satisfactory to the parties through use of labor arbitrators in whom the parties have confidence, and who possess special expertise in matters concerning productivity and worker morale, is equally applicable to safety disputes. The court of appeals expressed an unjustifiable fear that an arbitrator might not fairly appreciate the workers' interest in their own safety because "the parties are always free to choose an arbitrator whose knowledge and judgment they trust."

Having agreed to arbitrate the safety dispute, the United Mine Workers also impliedly guaranteed that they would not strike. The well-established Supreme Court rule of construction is that collective-bargaining agreements with broad mandatory arbitration provisions imply corresponding no-strike obligations in the absence of an express intent to the contrary. In this case, the agreement contained no provision clearly indicating that the union did not intend its implied no-strike obligation to cover the safety dispute in question.

The court of appeals also erroneously concluded that section 502 of the Labor Management Relations Act forbade the injunction against striking issued by the district court. That section provides that employees who in good faith quit work because of abnormally dangerous conditions shall not be deemed on strike. However, section 502 justifies a contractually permitted work stoppage only if the union presents "ascertainable, objective evidence supporting its conclusion that an abnormally dangerous condition for work exists." On the facts of this case, the required objective evidence under section 502 was lacking. The district court expressly conditioned injunctive relief on the suspension of the foremen in question pending decision by the arbitrator, thereby eliminating the allegedly dangerous working conditions. The Court thus upheld the district court decision enjoining the UMW strike and compelling arbitration of the alleged safety dispute.

National Labor Relations Board v. Bell Aerospace Co., 416 U.S. 267 (1974)

Facts: A labor union petitioned the National Labor Relations

Board to hold a representation election to determine whether the union would be certified as the bargaining representative of twenty-five buyers in the purchasing and procurement department at an aerospace company plant. The board held that the buyers constituted an appropriate unit for collective bargaining and directed an election. It reasoned that although the buyers might be characterized as "managerial employees," they were nevertheless entitled to unionize under the National Labor Relations Act, at least in the absence of proof that union membership would create a conflict of interest among the buyers. (The company contended that unionized buyers would favor purchasing goods and services from unionized sellers.) In reversing the board's decision, the court of appeals held that all "managerial employees" were excluded from the protections of the act and that the board was required to proceed by rulemaking (and not by adjudication) if it wished to depart from its earlier decisions holding that buyers were "managerial employees."

Questions: (1) Did the National Labor Relations Board properly conclude that all "managerial employees" are entitled to organize under the Labor Relations Act except those whose union membership would create a conflict of interest with job responsibilities? (2) Must the board proceed by rulemaking rather than by adjudication in determining whether certain buyers are "managerial employees"?

Decision: No to both questions. Opinion by Justice Powell. Vote: 5–4 on the first question, White, Brennan, Stewart, and Marshall dissenting, and 9–0 on the second.

Reasons: "Congress intended to exclude from the protections of the Act all employees properly classified as 'managerial.'" That conclusion is supported by the "Board's early decisions, the legislative history of the . . . [1947 amendments to the act], and subsequent Board and court decisions. . . ." The board's past decisions have defined "managerial employees" as those who " 'formulate and effectuate management policies by expressing and making operative the decisions of their employer.'" The case must be remanded to permit the board to determine whether the buyers were "managerial employees" and thus not entitled to unionize under the act.

Under principles of administrative law enunciated in *SEC* v. *Chenery Corp.*, 332 U.S. 194 (1947), the Court concluded that the board could proceed either by rulemaking or adjudication in determining whether certain buyers were "managerial employees." In *Chenery*, the Court rejected the contention that administrative agencies must proceed by rulemaking whenever establishing general standards to govern future conduct. It reasoned that

[p]roblems may rise in a case which the administrative agency could not reasonably foresee, problems which must be solved despite the absence of a relevant general rule. Or the agency may not have had sufficient experience with a particular problem to warrant rigidifying its tentative judgment into a hard and fast rule. *Or the problem may be so specialized and varying in nature as to be impossible of capture within the boundaries of a general rule.* In those situations, the agency must retain power to deal with the problems on a case-to-case basis if the administrative process is to be effective. There is thus a very definite place for the case-by-case evolution of statutory standards.

Beasley v. *Food Fair of North Carolina*, 416 U.S. 653 (1974)

Facts: Food Fair of North Carolina discharged certain supervisors because they joined a union. The discharged supervisors then brought suit for damages under North Carolina's right-to-work law which provides such an action for employees discharged on account of union membership. Food Fair successfully contended that enforcement of the North Carolina right-to-work law as applied to supervisors was barred by section 14(a) of the federal National Labor Relations Act. That section provides in part that "no employer . . . shall be compelled to deem individuals defined herein as supervisors as employees for the purpose of any law, either national or local, relating to collective bargaining."

Question: Does section 14(a) of the act prohibit enforcement of North Carolina's right-to-work law as applied to supervisors?

Decision: Yes. Opinion by Justice Brennan. Vote: 9–0.

Reasons: Under the Labor Relations Act, supervisors have no protection against discharge on account of union membership. The question in this case is whether the act should be interpreted to preclude North Carolina from affording supervisors its damage remedy for such discharges. The legislative history of section 14(a) and related sections compels the conclusion that its dominant purpose "was to redress a perceived imbalance in labor-management relationships that was found to arise from putting supervisors in the position of serving two masters with opposed interests. . . . We conclude therefore that the second clause of section 14(a) relieving the employer of obligations under 'any law, either National or local, relating to collective-bargaining' applies to any law that requires an employer 'to accord to the front line of management the anomalous status of employees'. . . . Enforcement against [Food Fair] in this case of

[North Carolina's right-to-work law] would plainly put pressure on [Food Fair] 'to accord to the front line of management the anomalous status of employees, and would therefore flout the national policy against compulsion upon employers from either federal or state agencies to treat supervisors as employees."

National Labor Relations Board v. Savair Mfg. Co., 414 U.S. 270 (1973)

Facts: For refusing to bargain with a newly elected union, an employer was charged with violating the National Labor Relations Act. As a defense before the National Labor Relations Board, the employer claimed that the union election was invalid. Prior to the election, union "recognition slips" were circulated among employees who were told that if they signed those slips an unspecified union initiation fee would be waived if the union was approved. Employees who failed to sign those slips would have to pay the union initiation fees. The employer claimed that the union offer to waive initiation fees for those signing the pre-election "recognition slips" illegally interfered with the right of employees to refrain from union activity in violation of section 7 of the act. In rejecting that claim, the board reasoned that the challenged waiver was unlikely to influence the election because those otherwise basing opposition to the union on the long-term cost of union dues and fees would not change their vote to avoid paying a relatively small initiation fee.

Question: Does a union offer to waive initiation fees for only those employees signing pre-election recognition slips illegally interfere with the right to refrain from union activity under the Labor Relations Act and thus invalidate a union election?

Decision: Yes. Opinion by Justice Douglas. Vote: 6–3, White, Brennan, and Blackmun dissenting.

Reasons: The Court reasoned that "[w]hatever his true intentions, an employee who signs a recognition slip prior to an election is indicating to other workers that he supports the Union." It may encourage other employees to vote for the union. By waiving the initiation fee for those signing recognition slips, a union is thus able to buy employee endorsements during its election campaign. Moreover, employees who oppose the union may fear its retaliation, should it gain recognition, for failing to sign recognition slips.

> His outward manifestation of support must often serve as
> a useful campaign tool in the Union's hands to convince
> other employees to vote for the Union, if only because many

employees respect their co-workers' views on the unionization issue. By permitting the Union to offer to waive an
initiation fee for those employees signing a recognition slip
prior to the election, the Board allows the Union to buy endorsements and paint a false portrait of employee support
during its election campaign . . . . [Moreover, if] we respect,
as we must, the statutory right of employees to resist efforts
to unionize a plant, we cannot assume that unions exercising
powers are wholly benign towards their antagonists whether
they be nonunion protagonists or the employer.

Consequently, the Court concluded that the union offer to waive initiation fees interfered with the right to oppose unions under the
act and thus invalidated the successful union election.

William E. Arnold Co. v. Carpenters District Council of Jacksonville, 417 U.S. 12 (1974)

Facts: In breach of a no-strike clause in a collective bargaining
contract, a union struck its employer to force reassignment of work
which the employer had given to another union. Such a so-called
"jurisdictional strike" is arguably an unfair labor practice under section 8(b)(4)(i)(D) of the National Labor Relations Act (NLRA).
The employer brought suit in Florida state court to enjoin the strike
under section 301 of the Labor Management Relations Act, which
authorizes suits for violation of collective-bargaining contracts. The
Florida Supreme Court reversed a lower court's issuance of a temporary restraining order prohibiting the strike. It concluded that state
courts have no jurisdiction to enjoin a strike in violation of a "no-
strike" clause which is also arguably an unfair labor practice prohibited by federal law.

Question: Do state courts lack jurisdiction to enjoin a strike
in violation of a collective-bargaining agreement that arguably constitutes an unfair labor practice under the National Labor Relations
Act?

Decision: No. Opinion by Justice Brennan. Vote: 9–0.

Reasons: The court reasoned to the following conclusion:
When an activity is either arguably protected by section
8 of the NLRA, the preemption doctrine developed in *San
Diego Building Trades Council* v. *Garmon*, 359 U.S. 236
(1959), and its progeny, teaches that ordinarily "the States
as well as the federal courts must defer to the exclusive
competence of the National Labor Relations Board if the
danger of state interference with national policy is to be

averted." When, however, the activity in question also constitutes a breach of a collective-bargaining agreement, the Board's authority "is not exclusive and does not destroy the jurisdiction of the courts in suits under section 301."

The exception to the *Garmon* rule is in recognition of the fundamental objective of federal labor law that the parties to a collective-bargaining agreement honor their contractual obligations. Accordingly, the state court had jurisdiction to entertain the employer's section 301 suit consistent with the congressional purpose that section 301 serve as the primary means to enforce "no-strike" clauses in collective-bargaining agreements.

Falk v. *Brennan*, 414 U.S. 190 (1973)

Facts: In a suit brought by the government under the Fair Labor Standards Act to compel the payment of minimum wages and overtime compensation, a real estate management company (Falk) defended on the grounds that it was not the employer of the employees involved and that it did business of less than $500 thousand during the relevant years, an amount required to trigger application of the provisions of the act. Falk managed several apartment complexes, performing virtually all management functions that are ordinarily required for their proper functioning. Employees of the owners were supervised by Falk but paid out of rentals received at the apartment complexes. Falk received gross commissions of slightly under $500 thousand in the relevant years, but the rents for all the buildings it managed exceeded $7 million. Falk contended that the involved employees were employed solely by the project owner and that its gross commissions rather than gross rents received was the proper measure of business done for purposes of measuring the $500 thousand minimum.

Questions: (1) Was Falk an employer of the project owner's employees for purposes of the Fair Labor Standards Act? (2) Under the act, was the proper measure of Falk's business done its gross commissions or the gross rentals collected?

Decision: Yes to the first question. Regarding the second question, gross commissions should be the measure of business done. Opinion by Justice Stewart. Vote: 9–0 on the first question, 5–4 on the second with Brennan, Douglas, White, and Marshall dissenting.

Reasons: The act defines "employer" as any person acting directly or indirectly in the interest of an employer in relation to an employee. Falk's managerial control and supervision over the project owner's employees made Falk an employer within the meaning of the act.

Regarding the second question, the act requires that the dollar volume of an enterprise be measured by the business it does. In this case, Falk's business is limited to the sale of its managerial services and thus the commissions it receives is the proper measure of business done. Falk does negotiate leases whose rents increase Falk's commissions which are determined as a percentage of gross rentals. But those rents do not constitute business done by Falk because its principal purpose in executing the leases is not the rental of property but the performance of managerial services.

Golden State Bottling Company, Inc. v. National Labor Relations Board, 414 U.S. 168 (1973)

Facts: All American Beverages, Inc. purchased Golden State Bottling Company, Inc. with knowledge that the National Labor Relations Board had ordered Golden State to reinstate with back pay a driver/salesman whose discharge was found to have been an unfair labor practice. In a subsequent proceeding, the board found that All American had continued to carry on Golden State's business without interruption or substantial changes in method of operation and was thus a "successor" to Golden State for purposes of the National Labor Relations Act. Accordingly, the board held Golden State liable for the reinstatement and back pay of the discharged driver/salesman. Golden State and All American sought review of the order claiming that it exceeded the board's remedial authority.

Question: Can the bona fide purchaser of a business, who acquires and continues the business with knowledge that his predecessor has committed an unfair labor practice in the discharge of an employee, be ordered by the Labor Relations Board to reinstate the employee with back pay?

Decision: Yes. Opinion by Justice Brennan. Vote: 9–0.

Reasons: The NLRB has authority under section 10(c) of the National Labor Relations Act to remedy unfair labor practices by ordering "such affirmative action including reinstatement of employees with or without back pay, as will effectuate the policies of this act. . . ." Section 10(c) thus authorizes the board to issue reinstatement and back pay orders against bona fide successors when the board has properly found such orders to be necessary to protect the public interest in effectuating the policies of the act. In this case, the board's order struck a balance between the conflicting legitimate interests of the bona fide successor, the public, and the affected employee. The board noted that whereas a successor could protect itself against unfair labor practice liability in negotiating the purchase price or securing an indemnity clause from the seller, a victimized employee would be without meaningful remedy if the successor was not liable for the wrongful discharge committed by the seller. The board's order against the "successor" All American in this case served to avoid labor strife, protect the victimized employee and deter unlawful discharges for union activity—all important policies of the act—and achieved at a relatively minimum cost to All American.

Florida Power and Light Co. v. International Brotherhood of Electrical Workers, Local 641, 417 U.S. 790 (1974)

Facts: Certain supervisory employees who belonged to a union crossed the union's picket lines during economic strikes and performed work normally performed by the nonsupervisory striking employees. Subsequently, the supervisory employees were found guilty of violating the union's constitution for their actions during the strike and received varying punishments including fines and expulsion from the union. The National Labor Relations Board ruled that the union's disciplinary action was an unfair labor practice under section 8(b)(1)(B) of the National Labor Relations Act. That section makes it an unfair labor practice for a union "to restrain or coerce . . . an employee in the selection of his representatives for the purpose of collective bargaining or the adjustment of grievances."

Question: Did the union's disciplinary action taken against the supervisory employees constitute an unfair labor practice under section 8(b)(1)(B) of the National Labor Relations Act?

Decision: No. Opinion by Justice Stewart. Vote: 5–4, Burger, White, Blackmun, and Rehnquist dissenting.

Reasons: Both the language and legislative history of section 8(b)(1)(B) compel the conclusion that a "union's discipline of one of its members who is a supervisory employee can constitute a violation of [that section] only when that discipline may adversely affect the supervisor's conduct in performing the duties of, and acting in his capacity as, grievance adjuster or collective bargainer on behalf of the employer." Because the supervisors in this case were disciplined for performing rank and file work during a strike and not for action taken in connection with grievance adjustment or collective bargaining, that discipline did not violate section 8(b)(1)(B). The Court noted that employers have the right under the act to ensure the full loyalty of supervisors during an economic strike by (1) refusing to hire union members as supervisors, (2) discharging supervisors for involvement in union activities, or (3) refusing to engage in collective bargaining with them.

National Labor Relations Board v. Magnavox Co. of Tennessee, 415 U.S. 322 (1974)

Facts: The National Labor Relations Board held that a company rule that prohibited unionized employees from distributing literature on all of its property, including parking lots and other nonwork areas, was an unfair labor practice under section 8(a)(1) of the National Labor Relations Act. That section prohibits, *inter alia,* company interference with employees' rights to form, join, or assist labor organizations. The company argued that because a collective-bargaining agreement with the union authorized its challenged rule, the rule should not be deemed an unfair labor practice, at least as applied to the prohibited literature in this case which was favorable to the incumbent union.

Question: Is it an unfair labor practice under section 8(a)(1) of the act for a company to prohibit the distribution of union literature in nonwork areas at all times, notwithstanding a collective-bargaining agreement permitting such prohibition?

Decision: Yes. Opinion by Justice Douglas. Vote: 6–3, Stewart, Powell, and Rehnquist dissenting in part.

Reasons: It has been firmly established that when alternative channels of communication are not available to employees (a fact not established in this case), a company may not prohibit the distribution of union literature in nonwork areas during nonworking time under section 8(a)(1) of the act. The sole question raised in this case is whether a union can waive employee rights of distribution and solicitation under section 8(a)(1) in a collective-bargaining agreement. The board concluded that the union possessed no such power to waive employee rights, whether or not those employees wished to support or oppose that union. That conclusion represents a proper exercise of the board's authority to "strike a balance among 'conflicting legitimate interests' which will 'effectuate national labor policy,' including those who support *versus* those who oppose the union."

Letter Carriers v. Austin, 418 U.S. 264 (1974)

Facts: During a drive to organize the remainder of letter carriers at a local post office, a union published a list of "scabs" together with a pejorative definition of that term. (The union had been selected as the collective-bargaining representative for the letter carriers pursuant to an executive order establishing procedures for unionization within the executive branch.) Three individuals named on the list successfully sued the union for defamation under state law. Over the union's objection, the trial judge ruled that the plaintiffs could recover if the challenged statements were "actuated by some sinister or corrupt motive . . . or . . . with such . . . recklessness as to amount to a wanton or wilful disregard of the plaintiff[s]." The union argued that federal labor law prohibits recovery for defamatory statements made in the course of a labor dispute unless the statements were false and made with knowledge of their falsity or with reckless disregard for the truth (actual malice). The union further contended that its challenged statements were made without actual malice and thus, that the defamation suits should have been dismissed.

Question: Should the defamation suits have been dismissed on the ground that the union's challenged defamatory statements were protected under applicable federal labor law?

Decision: Yes. Opinion by Justice Marshall. Vote: 6–3, Burger, Powell, and Rehnquist dissenting.

Reasons: In *Linn v. Plant Guard Workers Local 114*, 383 U.S. 53 (1966), the Court held that the National Labor Relations Act prohibited state defamation actions based upon statements made during labor disputes governed by the act unless the statements were made with actual malice. The rationale for *Linn* was the federal policy expressed in the act of encouraging free, robust, and uninhibited debate during labor disputes. In this case, the relevant law is an executive order governing labor relations in federal employment. Nevertheless, the provisions of that order clearly indicate that the same federal policies favoring uninhibited, robust, and wide-open debate in labor disputes under the act also apply to labor disputes arising under the order. Accordingly, state defamation actions based upon statements made during a labor dispute arising under an executive order and involving federal employees are barred unless the statements were made with actual malice.

It is argued that the challenged statements in this case were not made in the course of a "labor dispute," because they were made only in connection with the union's continuing organizational efforts after having achieved recognition. But "one of the primary reasons for the law's protection of union speech is to insure that union organizers are free to try to peacefully persuade other employees to join the union without inhibition or restraint. Accordingly, . . . any publication made during the course of union organizing efforts, which is arguably relevant to that organizational activity, is entitled to the protection of [the actual malice rule]." The challenged statements in this case were made during the union's organizing efforts and thus fell within the protection of the actual malice rule.

Naming as "scabs" the three individuals who refused to join the union was not done with actual malice. That statement was both literally and factually true. Only false statements of fact may provide a basis of recovery under the actual malice test. The challenged statements that defined "scab" pejoratively were only statements of opinions and likewise could not provide a basis for recovery.

Espinoza v. Farah Manufacturing Co., 414 U.S. 86 (1973)

Facts: A resident alien sued Farah Manufacturing Company under Title VII of the Civil Rights Act of 1964 contending that Farah's admitted refusal to employ her because she lacked United States citizenship violated section 703 of that act. A lower federal court ruled that section 703, which prohibits employment discrimination on the basis of "race, color, religion, sex, or national origin," did not prohibit discrimination based upon lack of citizenship.

Question: Does section 703 prohibit employment discrimination based on lack of citizenship?

Decision: No. Opinion by Justice Marshall. Vote: 8–1, Douglas dissenting.

Reasons: The legislative history of section 703 indicates that the phrase "national origin" was not intended to cover discrimination based upon lack of citizenship. Congress itself has on several occasions since 1964 enacted statutes barring aliens from federal employment. The Court refused to accept a contrary interpretation of section 703 embodied in a Federal Equal Employment Opportunity Commission guideline because that interpretation was "inconsistent with an obvious congressional intent. . . ."

Taxation, Antitrust, and Business Regulation

In the general area of taxation and business regulation, the Court's most notable decisions concerned antitrust, especially with regard to the potential competition theory. Generally speaking, the Clayton Act forbids mergers whose effect may be "substantially to lessen competition." Proving Clayton Act violations is necessarily difficult because it requires predicting the effect of a merger on competition in a changing trillion dollar economy. The Court has been criticized over the years for permitting proof of the anticompetitive effects of mergers and other business practices to rest more on speculation than upon hard economic evidence. During this term, the Court decided three important Clayton Act cases and indicated that it would require more hard evidence of potential anticompetitive effects to sustain challenges to mergers under the act than it had in past cases.

In a 5–4 decision, the Court sustained a district court finding that a merger of two coal companies which gave the surviving company some 23 percent of the market did not violate the Clayton Act, because there are special circumstances within the coal industry. In a 5–3 decision, the Court upheld the legality of a merger between commercial banks on the ground that the government failed to prove that the merger would eliminate potential competition. In that case, the Court stated that the potential competition doctrine embodies three elements of proof: first, that the market of the acquired company is substantially concentrated; second, that the acquiring company is perceived as a potential *de novo* entrant into the acquired company's market; third, that this perception of the acquiring company actually inhibits oligopolistic behavior by the existing participants in the relevant market. The Court indicated that proof of this third element required a showing that a *de novo* entry by the acquiring firm offered a substantial likelihood that the relevant market would be deconcentrated in the long term. Such a showing may be virtually impossible to make in many cases because of the difficulty in predicting long-term market behavior in the fluid and rapidly changing United States economy.

In the field of taxation, the Court produced no seminal doctrinal decisions. In accord with an earlier 1962 decision, the Court ruled that the collection of federal taxes could not be enjoined except in very extraordinary circumstances. The Court also held that state taxation of property in storage awaiting exportation was not barred by the import-export clause of the Constitution and that a 20 percent gross receipts tax levied upon commercial parking lot operators did not constitute an unconstitutional taking of property.

In other significant cases the Court ruled that the Federal Power Commission has no authority to deregulate the sale of natural gas and that CATV operators do not violate the Copyright Act when they intercept copyrighted television programs and rechannel them to paying subscribers. In a decision indicating a hostility toward unfair business practices, the Court upheld the constitutionality of state laws protecting trade secrets. It was argued that such laws were pre-empted by federal patent laws. The Court took a similar stance toward unethical business behavior last term in *Goldstein* v. *California*, 412 U.S. 546 (1972), when it narrowly construed the copyright clause of the Constitution and the federal Copyright Act to avoid preempting California's "tape piracy" statute.

Bob Jones University v. *Simon*, 416 U.S. 725 (1974)

Facts: Section 501(a) of the Internal Revenue Code exempts from federal income taxes certain organizations described in section 501 (c)(3). Section 501(c)(3) organizations are also exempt from federal social security taxes and federal unemployment taxes. Additionally, donations to section 501(c)(3) organizations are tax-deductible under section 170(c)(2). In 1970, the Internal Revenue Service (IRS) announced that it would no longer allow section 501(c)(3) status for private schools maintaining racially discriminatory admissions policies and that it would no longer treat contributions to such schools as tax-deductible. Thereafter, the Internal Revenue Service initiated administrative proceedings against Bob Jones University, a private school, to revoke its 501(c)(3) status, because it refused to admit Negroes as students. The university filed suit in federal district court to enjoin the administrative proceedings claiming that the IRS threatened action was unlawful and would violate the university's constitutional rights to freedom of religion, freedom of association, due process, and equal protection of the law. Additionally, the university alleged irreparable injury in the form of substantial federal income tax liability and the loss of contributions if injunctive relief were not granted. The Internal Revenue Service moved to dismiss the suit on the ground that it was barred by the Anti-Injunction Act, which provides that "no suit for the purpose of restraining the assessment or collection of any tax shall be maintained in any court. . . ."

Question: Was the university's suit seeking injunctive relief against the Internal Revenue Service barred by the Anti-Injunction Act?

Decision: Yes. Opinion by Justice Powell. Vote: 8–0. Douglas did not participate.

Reasons: The principal purpose of the act is to protect the "Government's need to assess and collect taxes as expeditiously as possible with a minimum of pre-enforcement judicial interference. . . ." Disputes over collected taxes are generally to be determined in a suit for refund. A collateral objective of the act is to protect the tax collector from litigation pending a refund suit. In furtherance of these goals, the Court held in *Enochs* v. *Williams Packing and Navigation Co.*, 370 U.S. 1 (1962), that the act barred injunctive relief unless (1) irreparable injury was proven, and (2) the government's legal position at the time of the suit was clearly untenable under any circumstances.

The university claims that the act is inapplicable in this case because its suit is not "for the purpose of restraining the assessment or collection of any tax. . . ." The university describes its purpose as the continuing receipt of tax-deductible contributions and not the obstruction of revenue. However, the record clearly establishes that the suit seeks to restrain the collection of social security taxes, federal unemployment taxes, and the taxes from university donors.

The university also claims that to bar the injunctive relief sought in this case would deny it due process of law in light of the irreparable injury it will suffer pending some type of refund suit. "[A]lthough the congressional restriction to postenforcement review may place an organization claiming tax-exempt status in a precarious financial position, the problems presented do not rise to the level of constitutional infirmities, in light of the powerful governmental interests in protecting the administration of the tax system from premature judicial interference."

Accordingly, the interpretation of the act as established in *Williams Packing* governs this case. Because the university's constitutional claims are disputable, the suit did not satisfy the two-pronged test established in *Williams Packing* for avoiding application of the act.

Alexander v. *"Americans United" Inc.*, 416 U.S. 752 (1974)

Facts: In 1950, the Internal Revenue Service issued a ruling concluding that a religious nonprofit educational corporation qualified as a tax-exempt organization under the predecessor provision to section 501(c)(3) of the Internal Revenue Code of 1954. As a consequence, the agency treated contributions to the corporation as charitable deductions under the predecessor provision of section 170(c)(2) of the code. In 1969, the agency issued a ruling revoking the corporation's section 501(c)(3) status on the ground that it had devoted a substantial part of its activities to influence legislation [a disqualifying characteristic under section 501 (c)(3)]. It also ruled that the corporation was exempt from income taxation as a "social welfare" organization under section 501(c)(4) of the code. This change in tax status rendered the corporation liable for unemployment taxes under the code and destroyed its eligibility for tax-deductible contributions under section 170. Seeking declaratory and injunctive relief, the corporation sued the Internal Revenue Service alleging that revocation of its section 501(c)(3) status was erroneous or in violation of the First and Fifth Amendments. The agency moved to dismiss the suit on the ground that the declaratory and injunctive relief requested was forbidden by the Declaratory Judgment Act and the Anti-Injunction Act. The former statute bars issuance of a declaratory judgment in cases "with respect to Federal taxes" and the latter act prohibits suits "for the purpose of restraining the assessment or collection of any tax."

Question: Is the suit barred by the Declaratory Judgment Act and the Anti-Injunction Act?

Decision: Yes. Opinion by Justice Powell. Vote: 7–1, Blackmun dissenting. Douglas did not participate.

Reasons: Bob Jones University v. *Simon,* 416 U.S. 725 (1974), reaffirmed the interpretation of the Anti-Injunction Act made in *Enochs* v. *Williams Packing & Navigation,* 370 U.S. 1 (1962). Under that interpretation, the Anti-Injunction Act permits an injunction against the assessment or collection of taxes only (1) "if it is clear that under no circumstances could the Government ultimately prevail . . .," and (2) "if equity jurisdiction otherwise exists." The *Williams Packing* criteria clearly were not met in this case.

The court of appeals reasoned, however, that the injunctive relief sought was not barred because the suit in question was not for the purpose of "restraining the assessment or collection of any tax" within the meaning of the Anti-Injunction Act. It noted that the lawsuit (1) did not seek to enjoin the assessment or collection of the corporation's own taxes, (2) was not primarily intended to restrain the assessment or collection of taxes, and (3) provided the only adequate means by which the corporation could litigate its claims. These observations are either unsupported by the facts or irrelevant to the question of whether the suit fell within the proscriptions of the Anti-Injunction Act.

First, "a suit to enjoin the assessment or collection of anyone's taxes triggers the "prohibition of the act. Second, the obvious purpose of the suit was to restrain the collection and assessment of taxes from the corporation's contributors. Third, the corporation may litigate its claims in a refund action for federal unemployment taxes. Accordingly, the injunctive relief sought in this lawsuit fell within the prohibition of the act.

The Court also concluded that the bar to declaratory relief in cases "with respect to Federal taxes" in the Declaratory Judgment Act was at least coextensive with the bar to injunctive relief in the Anti-Injunction Act and that declaratory relief thus was unavailable.

Kosydar v. National Cash Register Co., 417 U.S. 62 (1974)

Facts: National Cash Register (NCR) maintained an Ohio warehouse which contained machines built to foreign buyers' specifications that were awaiting shipment abroad. The Ohio tax commission assessed a personal property tax upon the machines. The company successfully contended in the Ohio Supreme Court that its warehoused machines were exports and thus the tax violated the import-export clause of the Constitution, Article I, section 10, clause 2. That clause bars a state from taxing exports without the consent of Congress except to the extent "absolutely necessary for executing its inspection laws."

Question: Were the warehoused machines exports within the meaning of the import-export clause and thus constitutionally exempt from Ohio's personal property tax?

Decision: No. Opinion by Justice Stewart. Vote: 9–0.

Reasons: Coe v. Errol, 116 U.S. 517 (1886), established the proposition that a commodity does not become an export within the meaning of the import-export clause until it begins a "final movement for transportation from the State of origin to that of their destination." In this case, National Cash Register's machines were assessed for taxation while sitting in a warehouse awaiting shipment. "Title and possession were in NCR, payment had not yet been made by the putative purchasers, no export license had issued, and the machines were in the complete control of [NCR]. More important, there had simply been no movement of the goods—no shipment, and no commencement of the process of exportation." Accordingly, the machines at the time of the questioned tax assessment were not exports for purposes of the import-export clause. The fact that the machines almost certainly would be exported does not alter this conclusion.

City of Pittsburgh v. Alco Parking Corp., 417 U.S. 369 (1974)

Facts: A Pittsburgh ordinance places a 20 percent tax on the gross receipts of private commercial parking lot operators while in effect exempting competing publicly operated lots from the tax. The Supreme Court of Pennsylvania upheld the claim of several private operators that the tax constituted an unconstitutional taking of their private property without due process. The state court based its decision on the fact that the 20 percent gross receipts tax caused the majority of private parking lot operators to operate at a loss, at least in part because competing publicly operated lots were exempt from the tax.

Question: Does the Pittsburgh gross receipts tax ordinance deprive private parking lot operators of property without due process?

Decision: No. Opinion by Justice White. Vote: 9–0.

Reasons: Past Supreme Court decisions clearly hold that a tax does not violate due process " 'simply because its enforcement may or will result in restricting or even destroying particular occupations or businesses.' " That principle of due process applies whether or not the taxing authority competes with private persons subject to the tax "in a manner thought to be unfair by the judiciary." Accordingly, the Pennsylvania Supreme Court erred in striking down the challenged ordinance on the ground that it caused private lot operators to lose money and granted an unfair competitive advantage to publicly operated lots.

The Court also concluded that even assuming that an unreasonably high tax imposed upon private enterprise coupled with an exemption for competing public operations might violate due process in some circumstances, such circumstances were lacking in this case. The shortage of parking space in Pittsburgh, the Court noted, will enable private lot operators to pass the 20 percent gross receipts tax on to their customers. The burden of the tax thus will fall chiefly upon customers.

United States v. *General Dynamics Corp.,* 415 U.S. 486 (1974)

Facts: A 1959 merger in which Material Service Corporation, a deep-mining coal producer, acquired United Electric Coal Companies, a strip-mining coal producer, was challenged by the government as violative of section 7 of the Clayton Act. Section 7 prohibits mergers whose effect "in any line of commerce in any section of the country . . . may be substantially to lessen competition, or tend to create a monopoly." The main theory of the government's case was that the merger would probably lessen competition in the coal industry in Illinois, or, alternatively, in the Eastern Interior Coal Province Sales Area (composed of Illinois, Indiana, and parts of several other midwestern states). The district court found no section 7 violation. It based its conclusion on the following four findings: (1) The post–1959 reduction in coal producers from 144 to 39 in the relevant geographic market occurred not as the result of mergers but as the result of a change in the nature of the demand for coal. (2) The merged coal companies in this case were not in direct competition, because one was engaged in strip mining and the other in deep mining. (3) Except for sales to Commonwealth Edison, a large public utility, the merged coal companies would not have competed in the sale of coal to their normal customers if they had operated independently. (4) United Electric's coal reserves were so low that its potential to compete with other coal producers was steadily diminishing.

Question: Did the district court err in holding that the challenged merger did not violate section 7 of the Clayton Act?

Decision: No. Opinion by Justice Stewart. Vote: 5–4, Douglas, Brennan, White, and Marshall dissenting.

Reasons: The government sought to prove that the merger violated section 7 by statistical proof that the concentration of coal producers was increasing and that the merger materially enlarged the market share of the merged companies in Illinois or in the Eastern Interior Coal Province. The government showed, for example, that before the 1959 merger, Material Service Corporation and United Electric controlled 15.1 percent and 8.1 percent respectively of the Illinois coal market; after the merger, their combined market share was 23.3 percent. Statistics like these establish a prima facie violation of section 7 under antitrust principles set forth in *United States* v. *Philadelphia National Bank,* 374 U.S. 321 (1963), and *Brown Shoe Co.* v. *United States,* 370 U.S. 294 (1962).

However, the district court properly found that other pertinent factors affecting the coal industry not reflected in the government's statistics mandated a conclusion "that no substantial lessening of competition occurred or was threatened by the acquisition of United Electric." Those factors included the decline of coal as a fuel source in the economy, the increasing percentage of coal sold to electric utilities, and the increasing use of long-term requirements contracts in the sale of coal to utilities, under which coal producers promise to meet utilities' coal requirements over a long term at predetermined prices. The district court properly concluded that these facts showed that ownership of coal reserves was the best indication of competitive strength. Because United Electric owned small amounts of coal reserves and had no potential for acquiring future reserves in large quantity, it was a weak competitor in the coal market. The district court's findings thus fully substantiate its holding that United Electric's acquisition would not substantially lessen competition in violation of section 7. (Under rule 52(a) of the Federal Rules of Civil Procedure, a federal district court's findings of fact must be accepted by an appellate federal court unless "clearly erroneous.")

United States v. *Marine Bancorporation, Inc.,* 418 U.S. 602 (1974)

Facts: The United States brought a civil antitrust action against two commercial banks in Washington State claiming that a proposed merger between them would violate section 7 of the Clayton Act. That section prohibits mergers "in any line of commerce in any section of the country" which may "substantially . . . lessen competition, or . . . tend to create a monopoly." Washington state law places heavy restrictions on the formation of branch banks and prohibits multibank holding companies. Despite these restrictions, the United States based its case exclusively on the potential competition doctrine under section 7. It contended that if the merger were prohibited, the acquiring bank would find an alternate and more competitive means for entering the market area of the acquired bank, and that the acquired bank would become an actual competitor of the acquiring bank through internal expansion or mergers. The government further contended that the merger would terminate the allegedly procompetitive influence that the acquiring bank was exerting on banks in the market area of the acquired bank because of its potential for entry into that market. The district court ruled against the government on all aspects of the case.

Question: Is the challenged merger in violation of section 7 of the Clayton Act?

Decision: No. Opinion by Justice Powell. Vote: 5–3, Brennan, White, and Marshall dissenting. Douglas did not participate.

Reasons: "Determination of the relevant product and geographic markets is 'a necessary predicate' to deciding whether a merger contravenes the Clayton Act." The relevant product market in this case is commercial banking. The relevant geographic market is the metropolitan area surrounding the acquired bank. The government contends that the state is also an appropriate geographic market on the theory that the merger may trigger other mergers that may lead to domination by all banking in the state by a few large banks. That contention is rejected because it is well established that a proper geographic market is an "area in which the goods or services at issue are marketed to a significant degree by the acquired firm." The acquired bank in this case did not operate statewide.

United States v. *Falstaff Brewing Corp.*, 410 U.S. 526 (1973), indicates that the

> principal focus of the [potential competition] doctrine is on the likely effects of the premerger position of the acquiring firm on the fringe of the target market. In developing and applying the doctrine, the Court has recognized that a market extension merger may be unlawful if the target market is substantially concentrated, if the acquiring firm has the characteristics, capabilities, and economic incentive to render it a perceived potential *de novo* entrant, and if the acquiring firm's premerger presence on the fringe of the target market in fact tempered oligopolistic behavior on the part of existing participants in that market. . . . The elimination of such present procompetitive effects may render a merger unlawful under section 7. . . . [H]owever . . . application of the [potential competition] doctrine to commercial banking must take into account the unique federal and state regulatory restraints on entry into that line of commerce.

In this case, the potential competition doctrine applies because the government showed that the commercial banking market in the relevant geographic market was concentrated. Three banking organizations in that area controlled approximately 92 percent of total deposits. However, the doctrine also requires that the acquiring firm have other feasible means of entering the market and "that those means offer a substantial likelihood of ultimately producing deconcentration of that market or other significant procompetitive effects." In this case, state law substantially restricts the ability of the acquiring bank to enter the market of the acquired bank other than by merging. Additionally, the government "failed to demonstrate that [available] alternate means offer a reasonable prospect of long-term structural improvement or other benefits in the target market." These facts compel the conclusion that the acquiring bank did not exert any "meaningful procompetitive influence" over banks in the relevant geographic market. Accordingly, the challenged merger did not violate section 7 of the Clayton Act by eliminating potential competition.

The Court added that in states stringently limiting the ability of banks to branch or otherwise to expand internally, "in the absence of a likelihood of entrenchment, the potential competition doctrine— grounded as it is on relative freedom of entry on the part of the acquiring firm—will seldom bar a geographic market extension merger by a commercial bank."

United States v. Connecticut National Bank, 418 U.S. 656 (1974)

Facts: The United States brought a civil antitrust action in federal district court under section 7 of the Clayton Act challenging a proposed merger between two Connecticut banks. Section 7 forbids mergers "in any line of commerce in any section of the country . . . [that] may . . . substantially . . . lessen competition, or tend to create a monopoly." The government contended that the merger would eliminate significant potential competition in commercial banking in several areas of Connecticut. (See *United States* v. *Marine Bancorporation, Inc.*, 418 U.S. 602 (1974), for a discussion of the potential competition doctrine.) In rejecting the government's claims, the district court ruled that (1) the appropriate "line of commerce" (product market) within the meaning of section 7 included both commercial banks and savings banks, and (2) the relevant "section of the country" (geographic market) under that section was the state of Connecticut as a whole.

Question: Did the district court err in determining the relevant product and geographic markets by which to assess the competitive impact of the challenged merger under section 7 of the Clayton Act?

Decision: Yes. Opinion by Justice Powell. Vote: 5–4, Douglas, Brennan, White, and Marshall dissenting in part.

Reasons: Economic realities govern the determination of the relevant product market in a section 7 suit. In this case, the district court "overestimated the degree of competitive overlap that in fact exists between savings banks and commercial banks in Connecticut." Commercial banks account for virtually all commercial loans. "Moreover, commercial banks . . . offer credit-card plans, loans for securities purchases, trust services, investment services, computer and account services, and letters of credit. Savings banks do not." Lastly, unlike commercial banks, savings banks offer no checking accounts. Thus, the district court should have treated commercial banking as the relevant product market, because commercial banks offer a "cluster of products and services" that the savings banks do not.

With regard to the relevant geographic market, the district court erred in concluding that it encompassed the entire state because the acquiring and acquired banks neither compete nor operate statewide. "[T]he relevant geographic market of the acquired bank is the localized area in which that bank is in significant, direct competition with other banks, albeit not the acquiring bank. . . . [T]he geographic market must be delineated in a way that takes into account the local nature of the demand for most bank services." Accordingly, the case must be remanded to the district court to determine the proper local geographic market.

The Court expressly rejected both the government's contention that Standard Metropolitan Statistical Areas per se defined the relevant geographic market and the bank's argument that that market should be defined solely on the basis of towns.

Federal Power Commission v. Texaco, Inc., 417 U.S. 380 (1974)

Facts: The Federal Power Commission (FPC) issued an order authorizing small natural gas producers to sell gas at the market price, even if in excess of maximum rates set for large producers. The commission, however, asserted its intent to keep the price charged by small producers "just and reasonable" as required by sections 4 and 5 of the Natural Gas Act by regulating such sales in the course of regulating the rates of pipelines and large producers to whom the small producers sell their gas. A federal court of appeals declared the order invalid on the grounds that (1) indirect regulation of the price of natural gas sold by small producers was not permissible, and (2) the order did not insure that the prices charged by small natural gas producers would be "just and reasonable."

Questions: (1) Is the FPC order providing for indirect regulation of natural gas prices permitted under the Natural Gas Act? (2) Does the FPC order assure that the prices charged by small natural gas producers will be "just and reasonable" as required by that act?

Decision: Yes to the first question and no to the second. Opinion by Justice White. Vote: 8–0. Stewart did not participate.

Reasons: "The Act directs that all producer rates be just and reasonable but it does not specify the means by which that regulatory prescription is to be attained. That every rate of every natural gas company must be just and reasonable does not require that the cost of each company be ascertained and its rates fixed with respect to its own costs." Accordingly, the Federal Power Commission did not exceed "its powers by instituting a regime of indirect regulation of small producer rates." The challenged program of indirect regulation protects the consumer because pipelines purchasing gas from small producers are not permitted to pass on to their customers costs that are excessive.

With regard to the second question, the Natural Gas Act clearly does not authorize the Federal Power Commission to exempt small natural gas producers from the requirement that their rates be just and reasonable. The challenged commission order does not specifically state that the just and reasonable standard will be used to approve pipeline purchases from small producers. The order is so ambiguous in that regard that the case must be remanded to the commission for further proceedings, in which the order should be modified to clarify the method it intends to use to determine whether a given rate is just and reasonable. However, the legislative history of natural gas regulation makes clear that the "prevailing price in the market place cannot be the final measure of 'just and reasonable' rates . . . ."

Teleprompter Corp. v. Columbia Broadcasting System, Inc., 415 U.S. 394 (1974)

Facts: Several creators and producers of copyrighted television programs brought suit claiming that the defendants had infringed their copyrights by intercepting broadcast transmissions of copyrighted material and rechanneling these programs through various community antenna television (CATV) systems to paying subscribers. A lower federal court ruled that copyright infringement occurred when the cable television systems distributed signals to subscribers that were beyond the range of local antennas.

Question: Did the defendant community antenna television systems commit copyright infringement by distributing to their subscribers distant signals from broadcasters that were beyond the range of antennas located in the CATV community?

Decision: No. Opinion by Justice Stewart. Vote: 6–3, Burger, Douglas, and Blackmun dissenting.

Reasons: The Copyright Act of 1909, as amended, protects a copyright holder from, *inter alia*, unauthorized "performance" of the copyrighted material. The question here is whether the reception and transmission of "distant" broadcasting signals by a CATV system constitute a "performance" of a copyrighted work. In *Fortnightly Corp.* v. *United Artists Television Inc.*, 392 U.S. 390 (1968), the Court concluded that "CATV systems act only as an extension of a television set's function of converting into images and sounds the signals made available by the broadcasters to the public." Consequently, the Court held " 'that CATV operators, like viewers and unlike broadcasters, do not perform the programs that they receive and carry.' " The plaintiffs contend that *Fortnightly* should not govern this case because the defendants (1) imported signals that could not normally be received with current technology in the communities they served, (2) exercised elements of choice and selection in choosing which distant signals to import, and (3) adversely affected the economics and market structure of copyright licensing. However, none of these facts justifies departing from the *Fortnightly* conclusion that the function community antenna television plays in the total process of television broadcasting and reception is insufficient to constitute a "performance" within the meaning of the Copyright Act.

Kewanee Oil Co. v. *Bicron Corporation*, 416 U.S. 470 (1974)

Facts: As a condition of employment, individual employees of Harshaw Chemical Company agreed not to disclose confidential information or trade secrets. These employees subsequently left Harshaw to form their own competing company. Harshaw then brought suit in an Ohio federal district court alleging that its former employees were unlawfully using its trade secrets and seeking an injunction against further use. Applying Ohio trade secret law, the district court granted a permanent injunction against the disclosure or use by the former employees of twenty trade secrets claimed by Harshaw. The court of appeals reversed, concluding that Ohio's trade secret laws were preempted by federal patent laws.

Question: Are Ohio's trade secret laws preempted by federal patent laws?

Decision: No. Opinion by Chief Justice Burger. Vote: 6–2, Douglas and Brennan dissenting. Powell did not participate.

Reasons: Ohio law generally defines a trade secret as any device or information used in one's business which gives him a competitive advantage over others. Ohio law makes unlawful the disclosure of a trade secret by those who learn of it under an express or implied restriction of nondisclosure or nonuse, or by some improper means. However, a trade secret is not protected against discovery by fair and honest means. Federal patent law, in contrast, confers a seventeen-year monopoly upon processes or devices which meet certain conditions of novelty, utility, and nonobviousness.

Article I, section 8, clause 8 of the Constitution grants to the Congress the power "[t]o promote the Progress of Science and useful Arts, by securing for limited Times to Authors and Inventors the exclusive Right to their respective Writings and Discoveries. . . ."

Goldstein v. *California*, 412 U.S. 546 (1973), held that this clause by itself did not prohibit states from encouraging and protecting the use of certain musical writings within their borders by appropriate legislation. The reasoning of *Goldstein* compels the same conclusion with regard to state encouragement and protection of trade secrets relating to inventions. Accordingly, states may regulate in the area of patents and copyrights unless preempted by federal law in this area.

The test of federal preemption in this case is whether Ohio trade secret law frustrates the full purpose and objectives of the federal patent laws. The patent laws are designed to encourage inventors to risk enormous efforts to discover new products and processes by offering a seventeen-year monopoly on such inventions if a full and clear description of the invention is disclosed to the general public. Trade secret law aims to encourage invention and maintain a high standard of commercial ethics. As applied to subjects that would not be eligible for patent protection, trade secret law clearly does not conflict with the patent law. Regarding subjects that would be eligible for patent protection, whether the patent law objective of disclosure as the quid pro quo of the monopoly protection granted can be reconciled with trade secret law must be considered. In this connection, three categories of trade secrets may be distinguished: " '(1) the trade secret believed by its owner to constitute a validly patentable invention; (2) the trade secret known to its owner not to be so patentable; and (3) the trade secret whose valid patentability is considered dubious.' "

As to the second category of trade secret, abolishing trade secret protection would not increase disclosure because the owner would not apply for patent protection in any event. Moreover, maintaining trade secret protection for this category would stimulate wider dissemination of the secrets through licensing arrangements that would not be possible without such protection.

Regarding the trade secret whose holder has a legitimate doubt as to its patentability, the risk of eventual invalidity by the courts may cause him to refrain from seeking a patent. However, the existence of trade secret protection would only marginally increase the number of such holders who would refrain from seeking a patent because "the potential rewards of patent protection are so far superior to those accruing to holders of trade secrets. . . ." Moreover, eliminating trade secret law for this category and thereby encouraging patent applications may increase the number of improperly granted patents. (Most patents challenged in court are invalidated.) Improperly granted patents restrict the use of ideas and inventions and thus.are contrary to the public's interest: "Eliminating trade secret law for the doubtfully patentable invention is thus likely to have deleterious effects on society and patent policy which we cannot say are balanced out by the speculative gain which might result from the encouragement of some inventors with doubtfully patentable inventions which deserve patent protection to come forward and apply for patents."

The federal interest in disclosure is greatest with regard to the category of trade secret information that is clearly patentable:

> If a State, through a system of protection, were to cause a substantial risk that holders of patentable inventions would not seek patents, but rather would rely on the state protection, we would be compelled to hold that such a system could not constitutionally continue to exist. In the case of trade secret law no reasonable risk of deterrence from patent application by those who can reasonably expect to be granted patents exists.
>
> Trade secret law provides far weaker protection in many respects than the patent law.

Accordingly, Ohio trade secret law is not preempted by the federal patent law.

INDEX OF CASES

Cover and Book Design: Pat Taylor

qp
4480